THE AMERICAN EXPLORERS SERIES

Narratives of the Career of Hernando de Soto in the Conquest of Florida

Vol I

AMS PRESS

NEW YORK

Narratives of the career of
Hernando de Soto
in the Conquest of Florida,
as told by a Knight of Elvas
and in a relation by Luys
Hernandez de Biedma, fac-
tor of the Expedition

TRANSLATED BY BUCKINGHAM SMITH
together with an account of
DE SOTO'S EXPEDITION

Based on the Diary of
RODRIGO RANJEL, his Private Secretary
translated from Oviedo's Historia General
y Natural de las Indias

EDITED WITH AN INTRODUCTION BY
Edward Gaylord Bourne
Professor of History in Yale University

ILLUSTRATED

IN TWO VOLUMES
Volume I

MCMXXII
ALLERTON BOOK CO.
New York

Library of Congress Cataloging in Publication Data

Bourne, Edward Gaylord, 1860-1908, ed.
   Narratives of the career of Hernando de Soto in
the conquest of Florida.

   (American explorers series)
   Original ed. issued in series: American explorers.
   1. Soto, Hernando de, 1500?-1542. I. Ranjel,
Rodrigo. II. Relaçam verdadeira. English. 1973.
III. Biedma, Luis Hernández de, 16th cent. Relacion
del suceso de la jornada. English. 1973.
IV. Oviedo y Valdés, Gonzalo Fernández de, 1478-
1557. Historia general y natural de las Indias.
Book 17, chapters 21-28. English. 1973. V. Title.
VI. Series: American explorers.

E125.S7B83 1973   973.1'6'0924 [B]   72-2823
ISBN 0-404-54902-0 (v. 1)

From the edition of 1922, New York
First AMS edition published in 1973
Manufactured in the United States of America

International Standard Book Number:
Complete Set: 0-404-54901-2
Volume One: 0-404-54902-0

AMS PRESS INC.
NEW YORK, N.Y. 10003

EDITOR'S INTRODUCTION

THE expeditions of De Soto and Coronado were the most elaborate efforts made by the Spaniards to explore the interior of North America, and in some respects they have never been surpassed in the later history of the country. Between them they nearly spanned the continent from Georgia to the Gulf of California. Of the two, that of De Soto excited the most interest at the time, and this distinction it still retains. It was the first extensive exploration of at least six of our Southern States, and their written history opens with the narratives which tell its story; these same narratives contain the earliest descriptions which we possess of the life and manners of the southern Indians so famous in literature and history—the Choctaws, the Cherokees, the Creeks, and the Seminoles; these narratives also record the discovery of the Mississippi River and the story of the first voyage upon it by Europeans.

Nor are these narratives less interesting in literary history. One of them—that accorded the first place in this edition—is the only considerable contribution in the Portu-

guese language, and by a Portuguese, to the
early history of the United States. In making another, a descendant of the Incas of Peru
transmuted the tale of hardships and meetings
with the Indians, friendly and hostile, into an
old romance of chivalry,—the first and certainly the most celebrated one dealing with an
American theme,—in which a groundwork of
fact is richly embroidered by the author's im-
agination with romantic details into a whole
so full of charm as to have beguiled even pro-
fessed historians. Finally, in contrast to this
quaint compound of knight-errantry and Indian fighting, we have a plain, unvarnished
account of what actually took place from day
to day from the hand of De Soto's private secretary, Rodrigo Ranjel. This last is now
made accessible, in English, for the first time
in this edition.

The earliest narrative of De Soto's expedition to be published was drawn up by one
of the Portuguese gentlemen who joined it
from the town of Elvas, which lies just
across the boundary from the Spanish city of
Badajos, where De Soto was well known.
The writer did not reveal his name, and his
identity has never been discovered. His *True
Relation,* as he entitled it, was published in
Evora, Portugal, in 1557. It was brought to
the attention of a wider public by the ever

alert and energetic Richard Hakluyt, who, in 1609, to promote the interests of the newly founded Virginia colony, translated it into English under the title: *Virginia richly valued by the description of the maine land of Florida her next neighbour; out of foure yeeres continuall travell and discoverie for above one thousand miles east and west, of Don Ferdinando de Soto, and six hundred able men in his companie. Wherein are truly observed the riches and fertilitie of those parts abounding with things necessarie, pleasant, and profitable for the life of man; with the nature and dispositions of the inhabitants. Written by a Portugall gentleman of Elvas, emploied in all the action, and translated out of Portuguese by Richard Hakluyt.* Two years later, with the same purpose in view, Hakluyt published a new edition of his version, changing the title to *The Discovery and Conquest of Terra Florida by Don Ferdinando de Soto and six hundred Spaniards his followers,* etc. This narrative, from its sobriety of tone, its nearness in time to the events which its author relates as an eye-witness, and the numerous indications that in its preparation he utilized memoranda made at the time, has generally been recognized by historians as the most trustworthy detailed account of De Soto's expedition that we have.

Next in order of publication and equal in fame comes: *La Florida del Inca. Historia del Adelantado, Hernando de Soto, Governado, y Capitan General del Reino de la Florida. Y de otros heroicos caballeros, Españoles, e Indios. Escrita por el Inca Garcilaso de la Vega, capitan de su magestad, natural de la gran ciudad del Cozco, cabeça de los reinos y provincias del Peru,* etc. (Lisbon, 1605, and again, Madrid, 1722.) Garcilaso was born in Cuzco, Peru, in 1537. He was the son of a Spanish officer of the same name, and of the sister of the last Inca, Huayna Capac. While a boy in Peru he knew personally many of the followers of De Soto, who came thither to recover their fortunes.[1] In 1560 he went to Spain, and there, about the year 1567, became more or less intimately acquainted with a gentleman who was a survivor of the expedition, and from whom he often heard of the exploits of the Spaniards and the Indians. Garcilaso, with the blood of both races flowing in his veins, felt doubly drawn to rescue from oblivion such heroic deeds. Of the existence of the narrative of the " Gentleman of Elvas " he makes no mention.[2] Finally after the lapse

[1] *La Florida*, 264.

[2] Yet Pedro Fernandez del Pulgar, who wrote the continuation of Herrera, declares that Gar-

of twenty years he persuaded his friend to tell him the story in course while he wrote it down. This took place about 1587,[3] forty-four years after the return of the expedition.

Garcilaso nowhere reveals the name of this friend, and no one, so far as I am aware, has attempted to determine his identity. Yet I venture to conjecture that he was the cavalier named Gonçalo Silvestre, whose experiences in the expedition are narrated in considerable detail. In fact, in Garcilaso's narrative only De Soto himself, his successor, Luis de Moscoso, and Juan de Añasco receive as frequent notice as Gonçalo Silvestre, who is not even mentioned by the "Gentleman of Elvas." After the expedition was over Gonçalo Silvestre went to Peru. About the year 1555 he returned to Spain in poverty.[4]

cilaso followed the Portuguese narrative. (*Proemio* of Gabriel Daza de Cardenas to the ed. of 1722.) Jared Sparks held the same view. (*Life of Marquette,* 289.) Neither writer advanced any proofs.

[3] *Cf.* the letter of Garcilaso of March 12, 1587, quoted in the *Proemio* of the edition of 1722, and the statement in Garcilaso's preface that he wrote it after the publication of his version of the dialogues of Leon Hebreo (1590), and, also, that on p. 190 of his text, that he was copying it in 1591.

[4] Nothing is known of Silvestre except what Garcilaso tells us in his *La Florida* and *Historia General del Peru.* Yet, he there supplies enough to enable Mr. R. B. C. Graham to write an account

After Garcilaso had finished his main narrative he incorporated in it supplementary paragraphs from two short accounts put together several years after the events by two soldiers, Alonso de Carmona and Juan Coles. These were rambling recollections, and the first did not observe the order of time or mention regions by name except in rare cases. Garcilaso submitted his completed work to a "Chronicler of his Catholic Majesty," who wrote him that he had compared it with a narrative in his own possession drawn up by a Spaniard who had been on the expedition for Mendoza, the viceroy of New Spain, and found that they were in harmony.[5] This chronicler no doubt was Antonio de Herrera, appointed to that position in 1592, and he testified to his approval of Garcilaso's work by making it the basis of his own account of De Soto in his *Historia General de las Indias*.[6]

Garcilaso's *La Florida* has never been translated into English in full, but Theodore Irv-

of his adventures, filling some seventy pages of his *De Soto*. Cf. Graham (*Hernando de Soto,* 201-272).

[5] For these facts see Garcilaso's preface.

[6] Cf. Theodore Irving (*Conquest of Florida,* viii.) and Shea (Winsor, *Narr. and Crit. Hist.* II. 290). Herrara explicitly asserted that he derived his material from another narrative. Dec.

ing's *The Conquest of Florida* reproduces the substance of it, and often the very words. Barnard Shipp, it is true, included in his *History of Hernando de Soto and Florida* an English rendering of the French version by Pierre Richelet, but without intimating that Richelet had adapted rather than translated Garcilaso, reducing the bulk of his work by about two-fifths. Miss Grace King's *De Soto and his Men in the Land of Florida* (1898) is in the main a reproduction of Garcilaso's *La Florida,* and preserves the atmosphere of romance characteristic of the original. Theodore Irving and Miss King both made use of the Portuguese narrative for supplementary material, but on the whole their works as history stand and fall with the historical character of Garcilaso's *La Florida.* The same is true, although to a somewhat less degree, of R. B. Cunninghame Graham's *Hernando De Soto* (1903). This author, while mainly depending on Garcilaso, has made more use of the Portuguese narrative and the other sources presently to be mentioned than was the case

VII. lib. VII. cap. XII. Yet Irving is obviously right in his assertion, as any one can see by comparing Herrera's account with the text of *La Florida.* Probably Herrera did have another brief source, and did not care to acknowledge the extent to which he had exploited Garcilaso's work, submitted to him in a friendly way.

with Miss King. Mr. Graham's book is seasoned with a dry humour which gives it a place quite its own in the De Soto literature.

Somewhat more than a half a century ago two new and important sources were brought to light. The first was the official report of the expedition by the King's factor, Hernandez de Biedma, which was drawn up in 1544. This was first published in 1841 by the French scholar Ternaux-Compans in a French translation. English versions soon appeared in B. F. French's *Historical Collections of Louisiana* (1850), and in W. B. Rye's edition for the Hakluyt Society of Hakluyt's translation of the " Gentleman of Elvas " (1851). In 1857 Buckingham Smith published the Spanish text of De Biedma's report in his *Coleccion de varios Documentos para la Historia de la Florida,* and seven years later he published an English translation from the original, together with a new translation of the Portuguese narrative.

In the meantime the publication of the previously inedited portions of Oviedo's *Historia General y Natural de las Indias* in a new and complete edition of that work revealed an entirely new contemporary account of De Soto's expedition, to which Buckingham Smith called attention in a casual and inconspicuous way in the introduction to his *Narratives of the*

Career of Hernando de Soto (1866). Twenty years later John Gilmary Shea, in his brief but critical survey of De Soto's expedition prepared for Justin Winsor's *Narrative and Critical History of America,* made considerable use of Oviedo's narrative; and in his essay on the sources he remarks that it was based on the report of the expedition which De Soto's private secretary prepared after his return, from a diary which he had kept. The next writer to call particular attention to this source was Mr. Woodbury Lowery, in his scholarly history of *The Spanish Settlements Within the Present Limits of the United States,* 1513-1561 (1901).[7] Mr. Lowery, however, neglected to mention the important fact that Rodrigo Ranjel, from whom Oviedo derived his materials, was De Soto's private secretary.[8]

[7] Mr. Lowery says that the latter part of the Ranjel narrative "follows very closely the Elvas narrative," thus implying that it was dependent upon it. I am unable to assent to this conclusion. The narratives are in general agreement, as is to be expected, if both are contemporary; but there are also considerable differences. That one is derived from the other is very unlikely. Oviedo died in the summer of 1557 at 79 years of age, and this was the year in which the Elvas narrative was printed.

[8] This is established by the following clause in De Soto's will: "Also, I order that to Rodrigo

My attention was arrested by Shea's remarks upon the source of Oviedo's narrative last spring when engaged in preparing a brief sketch of De Soto's expedition for my *Spain in America*. A subsequent careful examination of Oviedo's account convinced me that it contained embedded in it Rodrigo Ranjel's journal exactly in the same way as Columbus's journal of his second voyage has been preserved to us substantially complete by Las Casas in his *Historia de las Indias,*[9] and just as Herrera incorporated large blocks of Las Casas's unpublished narrative in his own history. The practice was a very common one in those days, and a penetrating criticism will bring to light in the future many historical sources of the first importance which have been preserved to us safely encased in some secondary narrative, whose authors found that copying answered their purpose quite as well, if not better than, recasting. In the present instance we have an account of De Soto's expedition in exact chronological order from the departure from Cuba to the entering into winter quar-

Rangel, my secretary, be given, for the good service he has rendered me, three hundred ducats of my goods." B. Smith (*Narratives of the Career of Hernando de Soto,* 277).

[9] *Cf.* Lollis's attempt to reconstruct Columbus's journal of his second voyage in the *Raccolta Colombiana,* part I. vol. I.

ters at Utiangüe,[10] November 2, 1541. In the main the language of the daily record was preserved, and is easily distinguishable and detached by the critical reader from Oviedo's editorial comments. In some places words are used which Oviedo explains in a parenthesis or footnote.

A comparison of the derivation and genesis of our other sources with the derivation and origin of this narrative in Oviedo's *History* must establish the last as fully equal in value and importance, so far as it goes, to the Narrative of the Gentleman of Elvas, and superior to the other sources regarding De Soto's great expedition. Garcilaso de la Vega constructed a narrative of some 240,000 words, rich in details, in romantic colouring, and in imaginary speeches, on the basis of the recollections after forty years of a Spanish knight who participated in the expedition, supplemented by the scanty, unsystematized memories of two soldiers. The " Gentleman of Elvas " based his account, published fifteen years later, on his recollections and upon memoranda taken at the time, which, notwithstanding his occasional mistakes in days and dates, must have been a fairly connected daily journal. Biedma's *Relacion* possesses the important ad-

[10] Called Autiamque by the " Gentleman of Elvas."

vantage of being the official report of a king's officer; but it is brief, and is given as a whole with comparatively few details, except as to directions and distances. In Ranjel's account the form and method and the presumable accuracy of the contemporary diary are preserved, and the material has been less worked over into a literary narrative than is the case with the account of the "Gentleman of Elvas."

The importance, then, of this Ranjel narrative for the history of the expedition and the criticism of our sources can hardly be overestimated. It enables the days' marches to be followed with an exactness hitherto impossible, and it therefore should greatly facilitate subsequent studies of De Soto's route. It also furnishes a gauge by which the romantic exaggerations and inventions of Garcilaso de la Vega can be measured and detected, and by which also the degree in which the anonymous "Gentleman of Elvas" had a daily record at his disposal. In the past, writers like Theodore Irving have argued that a Spaniard of high character and rank would be a more trustworthy authority than a foreigner like the unknown Portuguese. Such *a priori* criticism of these sources can no longer pass muster. Nor, on the other hand, is a scholar of the standing of Jared Sparks likely again to class the Portuguese narrative and *La Florida* of Garcilaso together, declaring that " both of the accounts are too romantic and vague for history "; [11] much less will a reviewer venture to write of " the apocryphal story of Hernando de Soto's overland expedition to the lower Mississippi,"[12] etc. The general trustworthiness of the *True Relation* (the " Gentleman of Elvas "), which from a literary point of view ranks among the best of the old exploration narratives, is powerfully reinforced by the journal of Rodrigo Ranjel.

In the present publication the object of the editor and the publishers, in accordance with the design of " The Trailmakers " series, has been to place within the reach of everyone interested in the subject the three most important contemporary sources relating to the expedition of De Soto. To get at the true history of this great enterprise has hitherto been no simple matter for readers who did not have access to large libraries: for all the earlier collections of the contemporary narratives are out of print and not easily obtain-

[11] *Life of Marquette,* American Biography, x. 289.
[12] Francis Bowen, in a review of Gayarré's *History of Louisiana* (North American Review, July, 1847, p. 6). Bowen was undoubtedly led to this extreme scepticism by the character of Garcilaso's *La Florida;* but, after all, his utterance deserves preservation as a curiosity of historical criticism.

able at a moderate cost; and all the popular detailed accounts now before the public reflect the unhistorical and romantic colouring of Garcilaso de la Vega.

In preparing this popular edition of the De Soto narratives Buckingham Smith's translation of the " Gentleman of Elvas " rather than Hakluyt's has been selected for several reasons. In the first place it is in the English of to-day. Some readers, no doubt, would prefer the old-time flavour of Hakluyt's Elizabethan English; but, on the other hand, the quaint and variable spelling and the obsolete words would perhaps be an impediment to a much larger number. Again, Hakluyt's translation, although not in print in any form at the present writing, can easily be found in the libraries in various forms, while Buckingham Smith's careful version has hitherto been accessible only in a very limited edition. Lastly, the thought that the more extensive circulation of the present volumes might make known to a wider circle the name and work of a Southern scholar who contributed not a little to our knowledge of the earlier history of the Spaniards in North America was not without its weight. Of the Biedma narrative Buckingham Smith's translation was selected because it is the only one made directly from the Spanish.

In the preparation of the translation of
the Ranjel narrative from Oviedo I have
aimed to supply an accurate and readable
version. In revising it I had the advantage
of consulting Dr. Charles P. Wagner, now
Instructor in Spanish at the University of
Michigan, who solved some perplexities and
pointed out some errors. In addition to
the Ranjel narrative I have translated several passages from Garcilaso's *La Florida* em-
bodying some of his quotations from the
memoirs of the two soldiers, Alonso de Carmona and Juan Coles. The collection con-
cludes with Buckingham Smith's life of De
Soto and his translation of De Soto's letter to
the municipal body of Santiago, Cuba, the only
extant communication from De Soto himself
in regard to the beginning of the expedition.
A few notes have been added to the Ranjel
narrative, but they have been restricted to
narrow limits. All the dates have been veri-
fied by comparison with the calendars of the
years 1539, 1540, 1541, and 1542, and all
the errors detected have been pointed out.
This process has effectively demonstrated that
the two narratives of " The Gentleman of
Elvas " and of Rodrigo Ranjel are based on
actual journals. That these daily records
were occasionally written up after the events
is indicated by such mistakes in the dates as

have been discovered, but that is something which happens in the case of most journals.

The reader who desires a fuller discussion of the route of the expedition will find the literature of the subject in Lowery's *Spanish Settlements*. Of the aspects of nature which met the eyes of these toiling Spaniards the classic *Travels through North and South Carolina, Georgia, East and West Florida,* etc., of the botanist, William Bartram, afford a rich and varied picture.

EDWARD GAYLORD BOURNE.

NEW HAVEN, *August,* 1904.

TRUE RELATION

OF THE

VICISSITUDES THAT ATTENDED

THE

GOVERNOR DON HERNANDO DE SOTO

AND SOME

NOBLES OF PORTUGAL IN THE DISCOVERY

OF THE

PROVINCE OF FLORIDA

NOW JUST GIVEN BY A

FIDALGO OF ELVAS

———

VIEWED BY THE LORD INQUISITOR

INDEX

OF THE CHAPTERS CONTAINED IN THE

DISCOVERY OF FLORIDA

VOL. I

CHAPTER I

PAGE

Who Soto was, and how he came to get the
Government of Florida   3

CHAPTER II

How Cabeca de Vaca arrived at Court, and
gave Account of the Country of Florida; and
of the Persons who assembled at Sevilla to
accompany Don Hernando de Soto   5

CHAPTER III

How the Portugues went to Sevilla, and thence
to Sanlúcar; and how the Captains were appointed over the Ships, and the People distributed among them   9

CHAPTER IIII

How the Adelantado with his People left Spain,
going to the Canary Islands, and afterward
arrived in the Antillas 11

INDEX OF CHAPTERS

CHAPTER V

PAGE

Of the Inhabitants there are in the City of Santiago and other Towns of the Island, the Character of the Soil, and of the Fruit . . . 12

CHAPTER VI

How the Governor sent Doña Ysabel with the Ships from Santiago to Havana, while he with some of the Men went thither by land . 16

CHAPTER VII

How we left Havana and came to Florida, and what other Matters took place 21

CHAPTER VIII

Of some Inroads that were made, and how a Christian was found who had been a long time in the possession of a Cacique 25

CHAPTER IX

How the Christian came to the Land of Florida, who he was, and of what passed at his Interview with the Governor 27

CHAPTER X

How the Governor, having sent the Ships to Cuba, marched Inland, leaving one hundred Men at the Port 34

CHAPTER XI

How the Governor arrived at Caliquen, and thence, taking the Cacique with him, came to Napetaca, where the Indians, attempting to rescue him, had many of their number killed and captured 38

INDEX OF CHAPTERS

CHAPTER XII

PAGE

How the Governor arrived at Palache, and was
informed that there was much Gold inland 45

CHAPTER XIII

How the Governor went from Apalache in
quest of Yupaha, and what befell him . . 51

CHAPTER XIIII

How the Governor left the Province of Patofa,
marching into a Desert Country, where he,
with his People, became exposed to great
Peril, and underwent severe Privation . . 59

CHAPTER XV

How the Governor went from Cutifachiqui in
quest of Coça, and what occurred to him on
the Journey 69

CHAPTER XVI

How the Governor left Chiaha, and, having
run a hazard of falling by the Hands of the
Indians at Acoste, escaped by his Address:
what occurred to him on the Route, and how
he came to Coça 78

CHAPTER XVII

Of how the Governor went from Coça to
Tastaluca 84

CHAPTER XVIII

How the Indians rose upon the Governor, and
what followed upon that Rising 92

INDEX OF CHAPTERS

CHAPTER XIX

PAGE

How the Governor set his Men in order of Battle, and entered the town of Mauilla . . 95

CHAPTER XX

How the Governor set out from Mauilla to go to Chicaça, and what befell him 98

CHAPTER XXI

How the Indians returned to attack the Christians, and how the Governor went to Alimamu, and they tarried to give him Battle in the Way 107

CHAPTER XXII

How the Governor went from Quizquiz, and thence to the River Grande 110

CHAPTER XXIII

How the Governor went from Aquixo to Casqui, and thence to Pacaha; and how this Country differs from the other 116

CHAPTER XXIIII

How the Cacique of Pacaha came in Peace, and he of Casqui, having absented himself, returned to excuse his Conduct; and how the Governor made Friendship between the Chiefs 123

CHAPTER XXV

How the Governor went from Pacaha to Aquiguate and to Coligoa, and came to Cayas . 129

INDEX OF CHAPTERS

CHAPTER XXVI

PAGE

How the Governor went to visit the Province of Tulla, and what happened to him . . . 135

CHAPTER XXVII

How the Governor went from Tulla to Autiamque, where he passed the Winter . . . 141

CHAPTER XXVIII

How the Governor went from Autiamque to Nilco, and thence to Guachoya 146

CHAPTER XXIX

The Message sent to Quigaltam, and the Answer brought back to the Governor, and what occurred the while 152

CHAPTER XXX

The Death of the Adelantado, Don Hernando de Soto, and how Luys Moscoso de Alvarado was chosen Governor 159

CHAPTER XXXI

How the Governor Luys de Moscoso left Guachoya and went to Chaguate, and thence to Aguacay 164

CHAPTER XXXII

How the Governor went from Aguacay to Naguatex, and what happened to him . . . 169

CHAPTER XXXIII

How the Cacique of Naguatex came to visit the Governor, and how the Governor went thence, and arrived at Nondacao 172

INDEX OF CHAPTERS

CHAPTER XXXIIII

PAGE

How the Governor marched from Nondacao to Soacatino and Guasco, passing through a Wilderness, whence, for want of a Guide and Interpreter, he retired to Nilco 176

CHAPTER XXXV

How the Christians returned to Nilco, and thence went to Minoya, where they prepared to build Vessels in which to leave Florida . 181

CHAPTER XXXVI

How Seven Brigantines were built, and the Christians took their Departure from Aminoya 186

CHAPTER XXXVII

How the Christians, on their Voyage, were attacked in the River, by the Indians of Quigualtam, and what happened 193

CHAPTER XXXVIII

How the Christians were Pursued by the Indians 198

CHAPTER XXXIX

How the Christians came to the Sea, what occurred then, and what befell them on the Voyage 202

CHAPTER XL

How the Brigantines lost Sight of each other in a Storm, and afterwards came together at a Kay 207

INDEX OF CHAPTERS

CHAPTER XLI

PAGE

How the Christians arrived at the River Panico 210

CHAPTER XLII

How the Christians came to Panico, and of
their Reception by the Inhabitants . . . 213

CHAPTER XLIII

The Favour the People found in the Viceroy
and Residents of Mexico 216

CHAPTER XLIIII

Which sets forth some of the Diversities and
Peculiarities of Florida; and the Fruit,
Birds, and Beasts of the Country 219

CONTENTS

(VOL. I)

                                                    PAGE

INTRODUCTION, EDWARD GAY-
    LORD BOURNE   v

TITLE PAGE OF A TRUE RELATION
    GIVEN BY A FIDALGO OF ELVAS xxiii

INDEX OF CHAPTERS xxv

EPIGRAM   1

DISCOVERY OF FLORIDA, THE TRUE
    RELATION BY A FIDALGO OF
    ELVAS*   3

*Originally published by the Bradford Club in 1866.

FERNANDO DA SILVERIA

Senhor da Serzedas, great Poet and very Illus-
trious, respecting the Material of this Book,
and in Praise of the Author.

EPIGRAM.

He who would see the New World,
The Golden Pole,* the second,
Other seas, other lands,
Achievements great, and wars,
And such things attempted
As alarm and give pleasure,
Strike terror and lend delight;—
Read of the author this pleasing story,
Where nothing fabulous is told,
All worthy of being esteemed,
Read, considered, used.

* We inhabit the Northern Arctic Pole, and that
people inhabit the Southern Antarctic Pole. Golden
Pole is used because the region is rich.

DISCOVERY OF FLORIDA

RELATION OF THE TOILS AND HARDSHIPS THAT
ATTENDED DON HERNANDO DE SOTO,
GOVERNOR OF FLORIDA, IN THE CON-
QUEST OF THAT COUNTRY; IN WHICH IS
SET FORTH WHO HE WAS, AND ALSO WHO
WERE OTHERS WITH HIM; CONTAINING
SOME ACCOUNT OF THE PECULIARITIES
AND DIVERSITIES OF THE COUNTRY, OF
ALL THAT THEY SAW AND OF WHAT
BEFELL THEM.[1]

CHAPTER I

WHO SOTO WAS, AND HOW HE CAME TO GET THE
GOVERNMENT OF FLORIDA.

HERNANDO DE SOTO was the son of an
esquire of Xeréz de Badajóz, and went to the
Indias of the Ocean Sea, belonging to Castilla,
at the time Pedrárias Dávila was the Gov-

[1] The original text is most accessible in the re-
print of it in the *Collecção de Opusculos Reim-
pressos Relativos a Historia das Navegações Via-*

ernor. He had nothing more than blade and buckler: for his courage and good qualities Pedrárias appointed him to be captain of a troop of horse, and he went by his order with Hernando Pizarro to conquer Peru. According to the report of many persons who were there, he distinguished himself over all the captains and principal personages present, not only at the seizure of Atabalípa, lord of Peru, and in carrying the City of Cuzco, but at all other places wheresoever he went and found resistance. Hence, apart from his share in the treasure of Atabalípa, he got a good amount, bringing together in time, from portions falling to his lot, one hundred and eighty thousand cruzados, which he brought with him to Spain. Of this the Emperor borrowed a part, which was paid; six hundred thousand reals in duties on the silks of Granada, and the rest at the Casa de Contratacion.

In Sevilla, Soto employed a superintendent of household, an usher, pages, equerry, chamberlain, footmen, and all the other servants requisite for the establishment of a gentleman. Thence he went to Court, and while there was accompanied by Juan de Añasco of Sevilla, Luis Moscoso de Alvarado, Nuño de

gens e Conquistas dos Portuguezes pela Academia Real das Sciencias de Lisboa. Tomo I. Lisboa, 1875. (B.)

4

Tobár, and Juan Rodriguez Lobillo. All, except Añasco, came with him from Peru; and each brought fourteen or fifteen thousand cruzados. They went well and costly apparelled; and Soto, although by nature not profuse, as it was the first time he was to show himself at Court, spent largely, and went about closely attended by those I have named, by his dependents, and by many others who there came about him. He married Doña Ysabel de Bobadilla, daughter of Pedrárias Dávila, Count of Puñonrostro. The Emperor made him Governor of the Island of Cuba and Adelantado of Florida, with title of Marquis to a certain part of the territory he should conquer.

CHAPTER II

How CABEÇA DE VACA ARRIVED AT COURT, AND GAVE ACCOUNT OF THE COUNTRY OF FLORIDA; AND OF THE PERSONS WHO ASSEMBLED AT SEVILLA TO ACCOMPANY DON HERNANDO DE SOTO.

AFTER Don Hernando had obtained the concession, a fidalgo arrived at Court from the Indias, Cabeça de Vaca by name, who had been in Florida with Narvaez; and he stated how he with four others had escaped, taking the way to New Spain; that the Governor had been lost in the sea, and the rest were all dead.

He brought with him a written relation of adventures, which said in some places: Here I have seen this; and the rest which I saw I leave to confer of with His Majesty: generally, however, he described the poverty of the country, and spoke of the hardships he had undergone. Some of his kinsfolk, desirous of going to the Indias, strongly urged him to tell them whether he had seen any rich country in Florida or not; but he told them that he could not do so; because he and another (by name Orantes, who had remained in New Spain with the purpose of returning into Florida) had sworn not to divulge certain things which they had seen, lest some one might beg the government in advance of them, for which he had come to Spain; nevertheless, he gave them to understand that it was the richest country in the world.

Don Hernando de Soto was desirous that Cabeça de Vaca should go with him, and made him favourable proposals; but after they had come upon terms they disagreed, because the Adelantado would not give the money requisite to pay for a ship that the other had bought. Baltasar de Gallegos and Cristóbal de Espindola told Cabeça de Vaca, their kinsman, that as they had made up their minds to go to Florida, in consequence of what he had told them, they besought him to counsel them; to

6

which he replied, that the reason he did not
go was because he hoped to receive another
government, being reluctant to march under
the standard of another; that he had himself
come to solicit the conquest of Florida, and
though he found it had already been granted
to Don Hernando de Soto, yet, on account of
his oath, he could not divulge what they desired to know; nevertheless, he would advise
them to sell their estates and go—that in so
doing they would act wisely.

As soon as Cabeça de Vaca had an opportunity he spoke with the Emperor; and gave
him an account of all that he had gone through
with, seen, and could by any means ascertain.
Of this relation, made by word of mouth, the
Marquis of Astorga was informed. He determined at once to send his brother, Don
Antonio Osorio; and with him Francisco and
Garcia Osorio, two of his kinsmen, also made
ready to go. Don Antonio disposed of sixty
thousand reals income that he received of the
Church, and Francisco of a village of vassals
he owned in Campos. They joined the Adelantado at Seville, as did also Nuño de Tobár,
Luis de Moscoso, and Juan Rodriguez Lobillo.
Moscoso took two brothers; there went likewise Don Carlos, who had married the Governor's niece, and he carried her with him.
From Badajóz went Pedro Calderon, and

three kinsmen of the Adelantado: Arias Tinoco, Alonso Romo, and Diego Tinoco.

As Luis de Moscoso passed through Elvas, André de Vasconcelos spoke with him, and requested him to speak to Don Hernando de Soto in his behalf; and he gave him warrants, issued by the Marquis of Vilareal, conferring on him the captaincy of Ceuta, that he might show them; which when the Adelantado saw, and had informed himself of who he was, he wrote to him that he would favour him in and through all, and would give him a command in Florida. From Elvas went André de Vasconcelos, Fernan Pegado, Antonio Martinez Segurado, Men, Royz Pereyra, Ioam Cordeiro, Estevan Pegado, Bento Fernandez, Alvaro Fernandez; and from Salamanca, Jaen, Valencia, Albuquerque, and other parts of Spain, assembled many persons of noble extraction in Sevilla; so much so that many men of good condition, who had sold their lands, remained behind in Sanlúcar for want of shipping, when for known countries and rich it was usual to lack men: and the cause of this was what Cabeça de Vaca had told the Emperor, and given persons to understand who conversed with him respecting that country. He went for Governor to Rio de la Plata, but his kinsmen followed Soto.

Baltasar de Gallegos received the appointment of chief Castellan, and took with him his wife. He sold houses, vineyards, a rent of wheat, and ninety geiras of olive-field in the Xarafe of Sevilla. There went also many other persons of mark. The offices, being desired of many, were sought through powerful influence: the place of Factor was held by Antonio de Biedma, that of Comptroller by Juan de Añasco, and that of Treasurer by Juan Gayton, nephew of the Cardinal of Ciguenza.

CHAPTER III

How the Portugues went to Sevilla and thence to Sanlúcar; and how the Captains were appointed over the Ships, and the People distributed among them.

The Portugues left Elvas the 15th day of January, and came to Sevilla on the vespers of Saint Sebastian. They went to the residence of the Governor; and entering the court, over which were some galleries in which he stood, he came down and met them at the foot of the stairs, whence they returned with him; and he ordered chairs to be brought, in which they might be seated. André de Vasconcelos told him who he was, and who the others were; that they had all come to go with him, and aid in his enterprise. The Adelantado thanked him, and appeared well pleased with their coming and proffer. The table being already laid, he invited them to sit down; and while at dinner, he directed his major-domo to find lodgings for them near his house.

From Sevilla the Governor went to Sanlúcar, with all the people that were to go. He commanded a muster to be made, to which the Portugues turned out in polished armour, and the Castilians very showily, in silk over silk, pinked and slashed. As such luxury did not appear to him becoming on such occasion, he ordered a review to be called for the next day, when every man should appear with his arms; to which the Portugues came as at first; and the Governor set them in order near the standard borne by his ensign. The greater number of the Castilians were in very sorry and rusty shirts of mail; all wore steel caps or helmets, but had very poor lances. Some of them sought to get among the Portugues. Those that Soto liked and accepted of were passed, counted, and enlisted; six hundred men in all followed him to Florida. He had bought seven ships; and the necessary subsistence was already on board. He appointed captains, delivering to each of them his ship, with a roll of the people he was to take with him.

CHAPTER IIII

How the Adelantado with his People left Spain,
    going to the Canary Islands, and afterward
    arrived in the Antillas.

In the month of April, of the year 1538
of the Christian era, the Adelantado delivered
the vessels to their several captains, took for
himself a new ship, fast of sail, and gave
another to André de Vasconcelos, in which the
Portugues were to go. He passed over the
bar of Sanlúcar on Sunday, the morning of
Saint Lazarus, with great festivity, commanding the trumpets to be sounded and many
charges of artillery to be fired. With a favourable wind he sailed four days, when it
lulled, the calms continuing for eight days,
with such rolling sea that the ships made no
headway.

The fifteenth day after our departure we
came to Gomera, one of the Canaries, on
Easter Sunday, in the morning. The Governor of the Island was apparelled all in
white, cloak, jerkin, hose, shoes, and cap, so
that he looked like a governor of Gypsies. He
received the Adelantado with much pleasure,
lodging him well and the rest with him gra-
tuitously. To Doña Ysabel he gave a natural
daughter of his to be her waiting-maid. For

our money we got abundant provision of bread, wine, and meats, bringing off with us what was needful for the ships. Sunday following, eight days after arrival, we took our departure.

On Pentecost we came into the harbour of the City of Santiago, in Cuba of the Antillas. Directly a gentleman of the town sent to the seaside a splendid roan horse, well caparisoned, for the Governor to mount, and a mule for his wife; and all the horsemen and footmen in town at the time came out to receive him at the landing. He was well lodged, attentively visited and served by all the citizens. Quarters were furnished to every one without cost. Those who wished to go into the country were divided among the farm-houses, into squads of four and six persons, according to the several ability of the owners, who provided them with food.

CHAPTER V

Of the Inhabitants there are in the City of Santiago and other Towns of the Island,— The Character of the Soil and of the Fruit.

The City of Santiago consists of about eighty spacious and well-contrived dwellings. Some are built of stone and lime, covered with tiles: the greater part have the sides of board and the roofs of dried grass. There are extensive country seats, and on them many trees, which differ from those of Spain. The fig-tree bears fruit as big as the fist, yellow within and of little flavour: another tree with a delicious fruit, called anane, is of the shape and size of a small pine-apple, the skin of which being taken off, the pulp appears like a piece of curd. On the farms about in the country are other larger pines, of very agree-able and high flavour, produced on low trees that look like the aloe. Another tree yields a fruit called mamei, the size of a peach, by the islanders more esteemed than any other in the country. The guayaba is in the form of a filbert, and is the size of a fig. There is a tree, which is a stalk without any branch, the height of a lance, each leaf the length of a javelin, the fruit of the size and form of a cucumber, the bunch having twenty or thirty of them, with which the tree goes on bending down more and more as they grow: they are called plantanos in that country, are of good flavour, and will ripen after they are gathered, although they are better when they mature on the tree. The stalks yield fruit but once, when they are cut down, and others, which spring up at the butt, bear in the coming year. There is another fruit called batata, the sub-sistence of a multitude of people, principally slaves, and now grows in the Island of Ter-

ceira, belonging to this kingdom of Portugal.
It is produced in the earth, and looks like the
ynhame, with nearly the taste of chestnut.
The bread of the country is made from a root
that looks like the batata, the stalk of which
is like alder. The ground for planting is prepared in hillocks; into each are laid four or
five stalks, and a year and a half after they
have been set the crop is fit to be dug. Should
any one, mistaking the root for batata, eat any
of it, he is in imminent danger; as experience
has shown, in the case of a soldier, who died
instantly from swallowing a very little. The
roots being peeled and crushed, they are
squeezed in a sort of press; the juice that
flows has an offensive smell; the bread is of
little taste and less nourishment. The fruit
from Spain are figs and oranges, which are
produced the year round, the soil being very
rich and fertile.

There are numerous cattle and horses in
the country, which find fresh grass at all seasons. From the many wild cows and hogs,
the inhabitants everywhere are abundantly
supplied with meat. Out of the towns are
many fruits wild over the country; and, as it
sometimes happens, when a Christian misses
his way and is lost for fifteen or twenty days,
because of the many paths through the thick
woods made by the herds traversing to and

fro, he will live on fruit and on wild cabbage,
there being many and large palm-trees everywhere which yield nothing else available
beside.

The Island of Cuba is three hundred
leagues long from east to southeast, and in
places thirty, in others forty leagues from north
to south. There are six towns of Christians,
which are, Santiago, Baracoa, the Báyamo,
Puerto Principe, Sancti Spiritus, and Havana. They each have between thirty and
forty householders, except Santiago and Havana, which have some seventy or eighty
dwellings apiece. The towns have all a chap-
lain to hear confession, and a church in which
to say mass. In Santiago is a monastery of the
order of Saint Francis; it has few friars,
though well supported by tithes, as the country
is rich. The Church of Santiago is endowed,
has a cura, a prebend, and many priests, as
it is the church of the city which is the
metropolis.

Although the earth contains much gold,
there are few slaves to seek it, many having
destroyed themselves because of the hard usage
they receive from the Christians in the mines.
The overseer of Vasco Porcallo, a resident of
the Island, having understood that his slaves
intended to hang themselves, went with a cud-
gel in his hand and waited for them in the

place at which they were to meet, where he told them that they could do nothing, nor think of any thing, that he did not know beforehand; that he had come to hang himself with them, to the end that if he gave them a bad life in this world, a worse would he give them in that to come. This caused them to alter their purpose and return to obedience.

CHAPTER VI

How the Governor sent Doña Ysabel with the Ships from Santiago to Havana, while he with some of the Men went thither by Land.

THE Governor sent Don Carlos with the ships, in company with Doña Ysabel, to tarry for him at Havana, a port in the eastern end of the Island, one hundred and eighty leagues from Santiago. He and those that remained, having bought horses, set out on their journey, and at the end of twenty-five leagues came to Báyamo, the first town. They were lodged, as they arrived, in parties of four and six, where their food was given to them; and nothing was paid for any other thing than maize for the beasts; because the Governor at each town assessed tax on the tribute paid, and the labour done, by the Indians.

A deep river runs near Báyamo, larger than

the Guadiana, called Tanto. The monstrous alligators do harm in it sometimes to the Indians and animals in the crossing. In all the country there are no wolves, foxes, bears, lions, nor tigers: there are dogs in the woods, which have run wild from the houses, that feed upon the swine: there are snakes, the size of a man's thigh, and even bigger; but they are very sluggish and do no kind of injury. From that town to Puerto Principe there are fifty leagues. The roads throughout the Island are made by cutting out the undergrowth, which if neglected to be gone over, though only for a single year, the shrubs spring up in such manner that the ways disappear; and so numerous likewise are the paths made by cattle, that no one can travel without an Indian of the country for a guide, there being everywhere high and thick woods.

From Puerto Principe the Governor went by sea in a canoe to the estate of Vasco Porcallo, near the coast, to get news of Doña Ysabel, who, at the time, although not then known, was in a situation of distress, the ships having parted company, two or them being driven in sight of the coast of Florida, and all on board were suffering for lack of water and subsistence. The storm over, and the vessels come together, not knowing where they had been tossed, Cape San Antonio was described, an uninhabited part of the Island, where they got water; and at the end of forty days from the time of leaving Santiago, they arrived at Havana. The Governor presently received the news and hastened to meet Doña Ysabel. The troops that went by land, one hundred and fifty mounted men in number, not to be burdensome upon the Islanders, were divided into two squadrons, and marched to Sancti Spiritus, sixty leagues from Puerto Principe. The victual they carried was the caçabe bread I have spoken of, the nature of which is such that it directly dissolves from moisture; whence it happened that some ate meat and no bread for many days. They took dogs with them, and a man of the country, who hunted as they journeyed, and who killed the hogs at night found further necessary for provision where they stopped; so that they had abundant supply, both of beef and pork. They found immense annoyance from mosquitos, particularly in a lake called Bog of Pia, which they had much ado in crossing between midday and dark, it being more than half a league over, full half a bow-shot of the distance swimming, and all the rest of the way the water waist deep, having clams on the bottom that sorely cut the feet, for not a boot nor shoe sole was left entire at half way. The clothing and saddles were floated over in baskets of palm-leaf. In this time the insects came in great numbers and settled on the person where exposed, their bite raising lumps that smarted keenly, a single blow with the hand sufficing to kill so many that the blood would run over the arms and body. There was little rest at night, as happened also afterwards at like seasons and places.

They came to Sancti Spiritus, a town of thirty houses, near which passes a little river. The grounds are very fertile and pleasant, abundant in good oranges, citrons, and native fruit. Here one half the people were lodged; the other half went on twenty-five leagues farther, to a town of fifteen or twenty householders, called Trinidad. There is a hospital for the poor, the only one in the Island. They say the town was once the largest of any; and that before the Christians came into the country a ship sailing along the coast had in her a very sick man, who begged to be set on shore, which the captain directly ordered, and the vessel kept on her way. The inhabitants, finding him where he had been left, on that shore which had never yet been hunted up by Christians, carried him home, and took care of him until he was well. The Chief of the town gave him a daughter; and being at war with the country round about, through

the prowess and exertion of the Christian he
subdued and reduced to his control all the
people of Cuba. A long time after, when
Diego Velasquez went to conquer the Island,
whence he made the discovery of New Spain,
this man, then among the natives, brought
them, by his management, to obedience, and
put them under the rule of that Governor.

From Trinidad they travelled a distance of
eighty leagues without a town, and arrived
at Havana in the end of March. They found
the Governor there, and the rest of the people
who had come with him from Spain. He sent
Juan de Añasco in a caravel, with two pinnaces and fifty men, to explore the harbour
in Florida, who brought back two Indians
taken on the coast. In consequence, as much
because of the necessity of having them for
guides and interpreters, as because they said,
by signs, that there was much gold in Florida,
the Governor and all the company were
greatly rejoiced, and longed for the hour of
departure—that land appearing to them to be
the richest of any which until then had been
discovered.

CHAPTER VII

How we left Havana and came to Florida, and what other Matters took place.

BEFORE our departure, the Governor deprived Nuño de Tobár of the rank of Captain-General, and conferred it on a resident of Cuba, Vasco Porcallo de Figueroa, which caused the vessels to be well provisioned, he giving a great many hogs and loads of caçabe bread. That was done because Nuño de Tobár had made love to Doña Ysabel's waiting-maid, daughter of the Governor of Gomera; and though he had lost his place, yet, to return to Soto's favour, for she was with child by him, he took her to wife and went to Florida. Doña Ysabel remained, and with her the wife of Don Carlos, of Baltasar de Gallegos, and of Nuño de Tobár. The Governor left, as his lieutenant over the Island, Juan de Rojas, a fidalgo of Havana.

On Sunday, the 18th day of May, in the year 1539, the Adelantado sailed from Havana with a fleet of nine vessels, five of them ships, two caravels, two pinnaces; and he ran seven days with favourable weather. On the 25th of the month, being the festival of Espiritu Santo, the land was seen, and anchor cast a league from shore, because of the shoals. On

Friday, the 30th, the army landed in Florida, two leagues from the town of an Indian chief named Ucita. Two hundred and thirteen horses were set on shore, to unburden the ships, that they should draw the less water; the seamen only remained on board, who going up every day a little with the tide, the end of eight days brought them near to the town.

So soon as the people were come to land, the camp was pitched on the sea-side, nigh the bay, which goes up close to the town. Presently the Captain-General, Vasco Porcallo, taking seven horsemen with him, beat up the country half a league about, and discovered six Indians, who tried to resist him with arrows, the weapons they are accustomed to use. The horsemen killed two, and the four others escaped, the country being obstructed by bushes and ponds, in which the horses bogged and fell, with their riders, of weakness from the voyage. At night the Governor, with a hundred men in the pinnaces, came upon a deserted town; for, so soon as the Christians appeared in sight of land, they were descried, and all along on the coast many smokes were seen to rise, which the Indians make to warn one another. The next day, Luis de Moscoso, Master of the Camp, set the men in order. The horsemen he put in three squadrons—the vanguard, battalion, and rearward; and thus they marched that day and the next, compassing great creeks which run up from the bay; and on the first of June, being Trinity Sunday, they arrived at the town of Ucita, where the Governor tarried.

The town was of seven or eight houses, built of timber, and covered with palm-leaves. The Chief's house stood near the beach, upon a very high mount made by hand for defence; at the other end of the town was a temple, on the top of which perched a wooden fowl with gilded eyes, and within were found some pearls of small value, injured by fire, such as the Indians pierce for beads, much esteeming them, and string to wear about the neck and wrists. The Governor lodged in the house of the Chief, and with him Vasco Porcallo and Luis de Moscoso; in other houses, midway in the town, was lodged the Chief Castellan, Baltasar de Gallegos, where were set apart the provisions brought in the vessels. The rest of the dwellings, with the temple, were thrown down, and every mess of three or four soldiers made a cabin, wherein they lodged. The ground about was very fenny, and encumbered with dense thicket and high trees. The Governor ordered the woods to be felled the distance of a crossbow-shot around the place, that the horses might run, and the Christians have the advantage, should the Indians make an attack at night. In the paths, and at proper points, sentinels of foot-soldiers were set in couples, who watched by turns; the horsemen, going the rounds, were ready to support them should there be an alarm.

The Governor made four captains of horse-men and two of footmen: those of the horse were André de Vasconcelos, Pedro Calderon of Badajóz, and the two Cardeñosas his kins-men (Arias Tinoco and Alfonso Romo), also natives of Badajóz; those of the foot were Francisco Maldonado of Salamanca, and Juan Rodriguez Lobillo. While we were in this town of Ucita, the Indians which Juan de Añasco had taken on that coast, and were with the Governor as guides and interpreters, through the carelessness of two men who had charge of them, got away one night. For this the Governor felt very sorry, as did every one else; for some excursions had already been made, and no Indians could be taken, the country being of very high and thick woods, and in many places was marshy.

CHAPTER VIII

OF SOME INROADS THAT WERE MADE, AND HOW A
CHRISTIAN WAS FOUND WHO HAD BEEN A LONG
TIME IN THE POSSESSION OF A CACIQUE.

FROM the town of Ucita the Governor sent
the Chief Castellan, Baltasar de Gallegos, into
the country, with forty horsemen and eighty
footmen, to procure an Indian if possible. In
another direction he also sent, for the same
purpose, Captain Juan Rodriguez Lobillo,
with fifty infantry: the greater part were of
sword and buckler; the remainder were crossbow and gun men. The command of Lobillo
marched over a swampy land, where horses
could not travel; and, half a league from
camp, came upon some huts near a river. The
people in them plunged into the water; nevertheless, four women were secured; and twenty
warriors, who attacked our people, so pressed
us that we were forced to retire into camp.

The Indians are exceedingly ready with
their weapons, and so warlike and nimble,
that they have no fear of footmen; for if
these charge them they flee, and when they
turn their backs they are presently upon them.
They avoid nothing more easily than the flight
of an arrow. They never remain quiet, but
are continually running, traversing from place

to place, so that neither crossbow nor arquebuse can be aimed at them. Before a Christian
can make a single shot with either, an Indian
will discharge three or four arrows; and he
seldom misses of his object. Where the arrow
meets with no armour, it pierces as deeply
as the shaft from a crossbow. Their bows are
very perfect; the arrows are made of certain
canes, like reeds, very heavy, and so stiff
that one of them, when sharpened, will pass
through a target. Some are pointed with the
bone of a fish, sharp and like a chisel; others
with some stone like a point of diamond: of
such the greater number, when they strike
upon armour, break at the place the parts are
put together; those of cane split, and will
enter a shirt of mail, doing more injury than
when armed.

Juan Rodriguez Lobillo got back to camp
with six men wounded, of whom one died,
and he brought with him the four women
taken in the huts, or cabins. When Baltasar
de Gallegos came into the open field, he discovered ten or eleven Indians, among whom
was a Christian, naked and sun-burnt, his
arms tattooed after their manner, and he in
no respect differing from them. As soon as
the horsemen came in sight, they ran upon
the Indians, who fled, hiding themselves in a
thicket, though not before two or three of

them were overtaken and wounded. The Christian, seeing a horseman coming upon him with a lance, began to cry out: " Do not kill me, cavalier; I am a Christian! Do not slay these people; they have given me my life!" Directly he called to the Indians, putting them out of fear, when they left the wood and came to him. The horsemen took up the Christian and Indians behind them on their beasts, and, greatly rejoicing, got back to the Governor at nightfall. When he and the rest who had remained in camp heard the news, they were no less pleased than the others.

CHAPTER IX

How the Christian came to the Land of Florida, who he was, and of what passed at his Interview with the Governor.

THE name of the Christian was Juan Ortiz, a native of Sevilla, and of noble parentage. He had been twelve years among the Indians, having gone into the country with Pánphilo de Narvaez, and returned in the ships to the Island of Cuba, where the wife of the Governor remained; whence, by her command, he went back to Florida, with some twenty or thirty others, in a pinnace; and coming to the port in sight of the town, they saw a cane sticking upright in the ground, with a split in the top, holding a letter, which they supposed the Governor had left there, to give information of himself before marching into the interior. They asked it, to be given to them, of four or five Indians walking along the beach, who, by signs, bade them come to land for it, which Ortiz and another did, though contrary to the wishes of the others. No sooner had they got on shore, when many natives came out of the houses, and, drawing near, held them in such way that they could not escape. One, who would have defended himself, they slew on the spot; the other they seized by the hands, and took him to Ucita, their Chief. The people in the pinnace, unwilling to land, kept along the coast and returned to Cuba.

By command of Ucita, Juan Ortiz was bound hand and foot to four stakes, and laid upon scaffolding, beneath which a fire was kindled, that he might be burned; but a daughter of the Chief entreated that he might be spared. Though one Christian, she said, might do no good, certainly he could do no harm, and it would be an honour to have one for a captive; to which the father acceded, directing the injuries to be healed. When Ortiz got well, he was put to watching a temple, that the wolves, in the night-time, might not carry off the dead there, which charge he took in hand, having commended himself to God. One night they snatched away from him the body of a little child, son of a principal man; and, going after them, he threw a dart at the wolf that was escaping, which, feeling itself wounded, let go its hold, and went off to die; and he returned, without knowing what he had done in the dark. In the morning, finding the body of the little boy gone, he became very sober; and Ucita, when he heard what had happened, determined he should be killed; but having sent on the trail which Oritz pointed out as that the wolves had made, the body of the child was found, and a little farther on a dead wolf; at which circumstance the Chief became well pleased with the Christian, and satisfied with the guard he had kept, ever after taking much notice of him.

Three years having gone by since he had fallen into the hands of this Chief, there came another, named Mocoço, living two days' journey distant from that port, and burnt the town, when Ucita fled to one he had in another seaport, whereby Ortiz lost his occupation, and with it the favour of his master. The Indians are worshippers of the Devil, and it is their custom to make sacrifices of the blood and bodies of their people, or of those of any

other they can come by; and they affirm, too,
that when he would have them make an offering, he speaks, telling them that he is athirst,
and that they must sacrifice to him. The girl
who had delivered Ortiz from the fire, told
him how her father had the mind to sacrifice
him the next day, and that he must flee to
Mococo, who she knew would receive him
with regard, as she had heard that he had asked
for him, and said he would like to see him:
and as he knew not the way, she went half a
league out of town with him at dark, to put
him on the road, returning early so as not to
be missed.

Ortiz travelled all night, and in the morning came to a river, the boundary of the territory of Mococo, where he discovered two
men fishing. As this people were at war with
those of Ucita, and their languages different,
he did not know how he should be able to
tell them who he was, and why he came, or
make other explanation, that they might not
kill him as one of the enemy. It was not,
however, until he had come up to where their
arms were placed that he was discovered, when
they fled towards the town; and though he
called out to them to wait, that he would do
them no injury, they only ran the faster for
not understanding him. As they arrived,
shouting, many Indians came out of the town,

and began surrounding, in order to shoot him with their arrows, when he, finding himself pressed, took shelter behind trees, crying aloud that he was a Christian fled from Ucita, come to visit and serve Mocoço. At the moment, it pleased God that an Indian should come up, who, speaking the language, understood him and quieted the others, telling them what was said. Three or four ran to carry the news, when the Cacique, much gratified, came a quarter of a league on the way to receive him. He caused the Christian immediately to swear to him, according to the custom of his country, that he would not leave him for any other master; and, in return, he promised to show him much honour, and if at any time Christians should come to that land, he would let him go freely, and give him his permission to return to them, pledging his oath to this after the Indian usage.

Three years from that time, some people fishing out at sea, three leagues from land, brought news of having seen ships; when Mocoço, calling Ortiz, gave him permission to depart, who, taking leave, made all haste possible to the shore, where, finding no vessels, he supposed the story to be only a device of the Cacique to discover his inclination. In this way he remained with him nine years, having little hope of ever seeing Christians more; but no sooner had the arrival of the Governor in Florida taken place, when it was known to Mocoço, who directly told Ortiz that Christians were in the town of Ucita. The captive, thinking himself jested with, as he had supposed himself to be before, said that his thoughts no longer dwelt on his people, and that his only wish now was to serve him. Still the Cacique assured him that it was even as he stated, and gave him leave to go, telling him that if he did not, and the Christians should depart, he must not blame him, for he had fulfilled his promise.

Great was the joy of Ortiz at this news, though still doubtful of its truth; however, he thanked Mocoço, and went his way. A dozen principal Indians were sent to accompany him; and on their way to the port, they met Baltasar de Gallegos, in the manner that has been related. Arrived at the camp, the Governor ordered that apparel be given to him, good armour, and a fine horse. When asked if he knew of any country where there was either gold or silver, he said that he had not been ten leagues in any direction from where he lived; but that thirty leagues distant was a chief named Paracoxi, to whom Mocoço, Ucita, and all they that dwelt along the coast paid tribute, and that he perhaps had knowledge of some good country, as his land was better than theirs, being more fertile, abounding in maize. Hearing this, the Governor was well pleased, and said he only desired to find subsistence, that he might be enabled to go inland with safety; for that Florida was so wide, in some part or other of it, there could not fail to be a rich country. The Cacique of Mococo came to the port, and calling on the Governor, he thus spoke:

MOST HIGH AND POWERFUL CHIEF:

Though less able, I believe, to serve you than the least of these under your control, but with the wish to do more than even the greatest of them can accomplish, I appear before you in the full confidence of receiving your favour, as much so as though I deserved it, not in requital of the trifling service I rendered in setting free the Christian while he was in my power, which I did, not for the sake of my honour and of my promise, but because I hold that great men should be liberal. As much as in your bodily perfections you exceed all, and in your command over fine men are you superior to others, so in your nature are you equal to the full enjoyment of earthly things. The favour I hope for, great Lord, is that you will hold me to be your own, calling on me freely to do whatever may be your wish.

The Governor answered him, that although it were true, in freeing and sending him the Christian, he had done no more than to keep his word and preserve his honour, nevertheless he thanked him for an act so valuable, that there was no other for him that could be compared to it, and that, holding him henceforth to be a brother, he should in all, and through all, favour him. Then a shirt and some other articles of clothing were directed to be given to the Chief, who, thankfully receiving them, took leave and went to his town.

CHAPTER X

How the Governor, having sent the Ships to Cuba, marched Inland, leaving one Hundred Men at the Port.

From the port of Espiritu Santo, where the Governor was, he sent the Chief Castellan, with fifty cavalry and thirty or forty infantry, to the Province of Paracoxi, to observe the character of the country, inquire of that farther on, and to let him hear by message of what he should discover; he also sent the vessels to Cuba, that, at an appointed time, they might return with provisions. As the principal object of Vasco Porcallo de Figueroa in coming to Florida had been to get slaves for his plantation and mines, finding, after some incursions, that no seizures could be made, because of dense forest and extensive bogs, he determined to go back to Cuba; and in consequence of that resolution, there grew up such a difference between him and Soto, that neither of them treated nor spoke to the other kindly. Still, with words of courtesy, he asked permission of him to return, and took his leave.

Baltasar de Gallegos, having arrived at Paracoxi, thirty Indians came to him on the part of the absent Cacique, one of whom said: "King Paracoxi, lord of this Province, whose vassals we are, sends us to ask of you what it is you seek in his country, and in what he can serve you;" to which the Chief Castellan replied, that he much thanked the Cacique for his proffer, and bade them tell him to return to his town, where they would talk together of a peace and friendship he greatly desired to establish. They went off, and came again the next day, reporting that as their lord could not appear, being very unwell, they had come in his stead to see what might be wanted. They were asked if they had knowledge or information of any country where gold and silver might be found in plenty; to which they answered yes; that towards the sunset was a Province called Cale, the inhabitants of which were at war with those of territories where the greater portion of the year was summer, and where there was so much gold, that when

the people came to make war upon those of
Cale, they wore golden hats like casques.

As the Cacique had not come, Gallegos,
reflecting, suspected the message designed for
delay, that he might put himself in a condition of safety; and fearing that, if those men
were suffered to depart, they might never
return, he ordered them to be chained together, and sent the news to camp by eight
men on horseback. The Governor, hearing
what had passed, showed great pleasure, as
did the rest who were with him, believing
what the Indians said might be true. He
left thirty cavalry and seventy infantry at
the port, with provisions for two years, under
command of Captain Calderon, marching
with the others inland to Paracoxi; thence,
having united with the force already there,
he passed through a small town named Acela,
and came to another called Tocaste, whence
he advanced with fifty of foot and thirty horse
towards Cale; and having gone through an
untenanted town, some natives were seen in
a lake, to whom having spoken by an interpreter, they came out and gave him a guide.
From there he went to a river of powerful
current, in the midst of which was a tree,
whereon they made a bridge. Over this the
people passed in safety, the horses being crossed
swimming to a hawser, by which they were

drawn to the other bank, the first that entered the water having been drowned for the want of one.

The Governor sent two men on horseback, with word to those in the rear that they should advance rapidly, for that the way was becoming toilsome and the provisions were short. He came to Cale and found the town abandoned; but he seized three spies, and tarried there until the people should arrive, they travelling hungry and on bad roads, the country being very thin of maize, low, very wet, pondy, and thickly covered with trees. Where there were inhabitants, some water-cresses could be found, which they who arrived first would gather, and, cooking them in water with salt, ate them without other thing; and they who could get none, would seize the stalks of maize and eat them, the ear, being young, as yet containing no grain. Having come to the river, which the Governor had passed, they got cabbage from the low palmetto growing there, like that of Andalusia. There they were met by the messengers, who, reporting a great deal of maize in Cale, gave much satisfaction.

While the people should be coming up, the Governor ordered all the ripe grain in the fields, enough for three months, to be secured. In gathering it three Christians were slain.

One of two Indians who were made prisoners stated that seven days' journey distant was a large Province, abounding in maize, called Apalache. Presently, with fifty cavalry and sixty infantry, he set out from Cale, leaving Luis de Moscoso, the Field Marshal, in command, with directions not to move until he should be ordered. Up to that time, no one had been able to get servants who should make his bread; and the method being to beat out the maize in log mortars with a one-handed pestle of wood, some also sifting the flour afterward through their shirts of mail, the process was found so laborious, that many, rather than crush the grain, preferred to eat it parched and sodden. The mass was baked in clay dishes, set over fire, in the manner that I have described as done in Cuba.

CHAPTER XI

HOW THE GOVERNOR ARRIVED AT CALIQUEN, AND THENCE, TAKING THE CACIQUE WITH HIM, CAME TO NAPETACA, WHERE THE INDIANS, ATTEMPTING TO RESCUE HIM, HAD MANY OF THEIR NUMBER KILLED AND CAPTURED.

On the eleventh day of August, in the year 1539, the Governor left Cale, and arrived to sleep at a small town called Ytara, and the next day at another called Potano, and the

third at Utinama, and then at another named
Malapaz. This place was so called because
one, representing himself to be its Cacique,
came peacefully, saying that he wished to
serve the Governor with his people, and
asked that he would cause the twenty-eight
men and women, prisoners taken the night
before, to be set at liberty; that provisions
should be brought, and that he would furnish
a guide for the country in advance of us;
whereupon, the Governor having ordered the
prisoners to be let loose, and the Indian put
under guard, the next day in the morning
came many natives close to a scrub surrounding the town, near which the prisoner asked
to be taken, that he might speak and satisfy
them, as they would obey in whatever he
commanded; but no sooner had he found himself close to them, than he boldly started away,
and fled so swiftly that no one could overtake
him, going off with the rest into the woods.
The Governor ordered a bloodhound, already
fleshed upon him, to be let loose, which, passing by many, seized upon the faithless Cacique,
and held him until the Christians had come up.

From this town the people went to sleep
at the one of Cholupaha, which, for its
abundance of maize, received the name of
Villafarta; thence, crossing a river before it,
by a bridge they had made of wood, the Chris-

tians marched two days through an uninhabited country.

On the seventeenth day of August they
arrived at Caliquen, where they heard of the
Province of Apalache, of Narvaez having
been there and embarked, because no road was
to be found over which to go forward, and
of there being no other town, and that water
was on all sides. Every mind was depressed
at this information, and all counselled the
Governor to go back to the port, that they
might not be lost, as Narvaez had been, and
to leave the land of Florida; that, should
they go further, they might not be able to get
back, as the little maize that was yet left the
Indians would secuie: to which Soto replied,
that he would never return until he had seen
with his own eyes what was asserted, things
that to him appeared incredible. Then he
ordered us to be in readiness for the saddle,
sending word to Luis de Moscoso to advance
from Cale, that he waited for him; and, as
in the judgment of the Field Marshal, and
of many others, they should have to return
from Apalache, they buried in Cale some iron
implements with other things. They reached
Caliquen through much suffering; for the
land over which the Governor had marched
lay wasted and was without maize.

All the people having come up, a bridge was

ordered to be made over a river that passed
near the town, whereon we crossed, the tenth
day of September, taking with us the Cacique.
When three days on our journey, some
Indians arrived to visit their lord; and every
day they came out to the road, playing upon
flutes, a token among them that they come in
peace. They stated that further on there was
a Cacique named Uzachil, kinsman of the
Chief of Caliquen, their lord, who waited
the arrival of the Governor, prepared to do
great services; and they besought them to set
their Cacique free, which he feared to do, lest
they should go off without giving him any
guides; so he got rid of them from day to
day with specious excuses.

We marched five days, passing through
some small towns, and arrived at Napetaca on
the fifteenth day of September, where we
found fourteen or fifteen Indians who begged
for the release of the Cacique of Caliquen,
to whom the Governor declared that their
lord was no prisoner, his attendance being
wished only as far as Uzachil. Having
learned from Juan Ortiz, to whom a native
had made it known, that the Indians had determined to assemble and fall upon the Christians, for the recovery of their Chief, the
Governor, on the day for which the attack
was concerted, commanded his men to be in

readiness, the cavalry to be armed and on horseback, each one so disposed of in his lodge as not to be seen of the Indians, that they might come to the town without reserve. Four hundred warriors, with bows and arrows, appeared in sight of the camp; and, going into a thicket, they sent two of their number to demand the Cacique: the Governor, with six men on foot, taking the Chief by the hand, conversing with him the while to assure the Indians, went towards the place where they were, when, finding the moment propitious, he ordered a trumpet to be sounded: directly, they who were in the houses, foot as well as horse, set upon the natives, who, assailed unexpectedly, thought only of their safety. Of two horses killed, one was that of the Governor, who was mounted instantly on another. From thirty to forty natives fell by the lance; the rest escaped into two very large ponds, situated some way apart, wherein they swam about; and, being surrounded by the Christians, they were shot at with crossbow and arquebuse, although to no purpose, because of the long distance they were off.

At night, one of the lakes was ordered to be guarded, the people not being sufficient to encircle both. The Indians, in attempting to escape in the dark, would come swimming noiselessly to the shore, with a leaf of water-

lily on the head, that they might pass unob-
served; when those mounted, at sight of any
ruffle on the surface, would dash into the
water up to the breasts of the horses, and the
natives would again retire. In such way
passed the night, neither party taking any rest.
Juan Ortiz told them that, as escape was
impossible, they would do well to give up;
which they did, driven by extreme chillness of
the water; and one after another, as cold
overpowered, called out to him, asking not
to be killed—that he was coming straightway
to put himself in the hands of the Governor.
At four o'clock in the morning they had all
surrendered, save twelve of the principal men,
who, as of more distinction and valiant than
the rest, preferred to die rather than yield:
then the Indians of Paracoxi, who were going
about unshackled, went in after them, swimming, and pulled them out by the hair. They
were all put in chains, and, on the day following, were divided among the Christians
for their service.

While captives, these men determined to
rebel, and gave the lead to an interpreter, one
reputed brave, that when the Governor might
come near to speak with him, he should
strangle him; but no sooner was the occasion
presented, and before his hands could be
thrown about the neck of Soto, his purpose

was discovered, and he received so heavy a
blow from him in the nostrils, that they
gushed with blood. The Indians all rose
together. He who could only catch up a
pestle from a mortar, as well he who could
grasp a weapon, equally exerted himself to
kill his master, or the first one he met; and
he whose fortune it was to light on a lance,
or a sword, handled it in a manner as though
he had been accustomed to use it all his days.
One Indian, in the public yard of the town,
with blade in hand, fought like a bull in the
arena, until the halberdiers of the Governor,
arriving, put an end to him. Another got
up, with a lance, into a maize crib, made of
cane, called by Indians barbacoa, and defended
the entrance with the uproar of ten men,
until he was stricken down with a battle-
axe. They who were subdued may have been
in all two hundred men: some of the young-
est the Governor gave to those who had good
chains and were vigilant; all the rest were
ordered to execution, and, being bound to a
post in the middle of the town yard, they were
shot to death with arrows by the people of
Paracoxi.

CHAPTER XII

How the Governor arrived at Palache, and was informed that there was much Gold inland.

On the twenty-third day of September the Governor left Napetaca, and went to rest at a river, where two Indians brought him a deer from the Cacique of Uzachil; and the next day, having passed through a large town called Hapaluya, he slept at Uzachil. He found no person there; for the inhabitants, informed of the deaths at Napetaca, dared not remain. In the town was found their food, much maize, beans, and pumpkins, on which the Christians lived. The maize is like coarse millet; the pumpkins are better and more savoury than those of Spain.

Two captains having been sent in opposite directions, in quest of Indians, a hundred men and women were taken, one or two of whom were chosen out for the Governor, as was always customary for officers to do after successful inroads, dividing the others among themselves and companions. They were led off in chains, with collars about the neck, to carry luggage and grind corn, doing the labour proper to servants. Sometimes it happened that, going with them for wood or maize, they would kill the Christian, and flee, with the

chain on, which others would file at night
with a splinter of stone, in the place of iron,
at which work, when caught, they were punished, as a warning to others, and that they
might not do the like. The women and
youths, when removed a hundred leagues
from their country, no longer cared, and were
taken along loose, doing the work, and in a
very little time learning the Spanish language.

From Uzachil the Governor went towards
Apalache, and at the end of two days' travel
arrived at a town called Axille. After that,
the Indians having no knowledge of the
Christians, they were come upon unawares,
the greater part escaping, nevertheless, because
there were woods near town. The next day,
the first of October, the Governor took his
departure in the morning, and ordered a
bridge to be made over a river which he had
to cross. The depth there, for a stone's throw,
was over the head, and afterward the water
came to the waist, for the distance of a crossbow-shot, where was a growth of tall and
dense forest, into which the Indians came, to
ascertain if they could assail the men at work
and prevent a passage; but they were dispersed
by the arrival of crossbow-men, and some tim-
bers being thrown in, the men gained the
opposite side and secured the way. On the
fourth day of the week, Wednesday of St.

Francis, the Governor crossed over and reached Uitachuco, a town subject to Apalache, where he slept. He found it burning, the Indians having set it on fire.

Thenceforward the country was well inhabited, producing much corn, the way leading by many habitations like villages. Sunday, the twenty-fifth of October,[1] he arrived at the town of Uzela, and on Monday at Anhayca Apalache, where the lord of all that country and Province resided. The Campmaster, whose duty it is to divide and lodge the men, quartered them about the town, at the distance of half a league to a league apart. There were other towns which had much maize, pumpkins, beans, and dried plums of the country, whence were brought together at Anhayca Apalache what appeared to be sufficient provision for the winter. These *ameixas* are better than those of Spain, and come from trees that grow in the fields without being planted.

Informed that the sea was eight leagues distant, the Governor directly sent a captain thither, with cavalry and infantry, who found a town called Ochete, eight leagues on the way; and, coming to the coast, he saw where a great tree had been felled, the trunk split up

[1] October twenty-fifth, 1539, came on Saturday. (B.)

into stakes, and with the limbs made into mangers. He found also the skulls of horses. With these discoveries he returned, and what was said of Narvaez was believed to be certain, that he had there made boats, in which he left the country, and was lost in them at sea. Presently Juan de Añasco made ready to go to the port of Espiritu Santo, taking thirty cavalry, with orders from the Governor to Calderon, who had remained there, that he should abandon the town, and bring all the people to Apalache.

In Uzachil, and other towns on the way, Añasco found many people who had already become careless; still, to avoid detention, no captures were made, as it was not well to give the Indians sufficient time to come together. He went through the towns at night, stopping at a distance from the population for three or four hours, to rest, and at the end of ten days arrived at the port. He dispatched two caravels to Cuba, in which he sent to Doña Ysabel twenty women brought by him from Ytara and Potano, near Cale; and, taking with him the foot-soldiers in the brigantines, from point to point along the coast by sea, he went towards Palache. Calderon with the cavalry, and some crossbow-men of foot, went by land. The Indians at several places beset him, and wounded some of the men. On his

arrival, the Governor ordered planks and
spikes to be taken to the coast for building
a piragua, into which thirty men entered well
armed from the bay, going to and coming
from sea, waiting the arrival of the brigantines, and sometimes fighting with the natives,
who went up and down the estuary in canoes.
On Saturday, the twenty-ninth of November, in a high wind, an Indian passed through
the sentries undiscovered, and set fire to the
town, two portions of which, in consequence,
were instantly consumed.

On Sunday, the twenty-eighth of December,
Juan de Añasco arrived; and the Governor
directed Francisco Maldonado, Captain of
Infantry, to run the coast to the westward
with fifty men, and look for an entrance; pro-
posing to go himself in that direction by land
on discoveries. The same day, eight men rode
two leagues about the town in pursuit of
Indians, who had become so bold that they
would venture up within two crossbow-shot
of the camp to kill our people. Two were
discovered engaged in picking beans, and
might have escaped, but a woman being present, the wife of one of them, they stood to
fight. Before they could be killed, three
horses were wounded, one of which died in
a few days. Calderon going along the coast
near by, the Indians came out against him

from a wood, driving him from his course, and capturing from many of his company a part of their indispensable subsistence.

Three or four days having elapsed beyond the time set for the going and return of Maldonado, the Governor resolved that, should he not appear at the end of eight days, he would go thence and wait no longer; when the Captain arrived, bringing with him an Indian from a Province called Ochus, sixty leagues from Apalache, and the news of having found a sheltered port with a good depth of water. The Governor was highly pleased, hoping to find a good country ahead; and he sent Maldonado to Havana for provisions, with which to meet him at that port of his discovery, to which he would himself come by land; but should he not reach there that summer, then he directed him to go back to Havana and return there the next season to await him, as he would make it his express object to march in quest of Ochus.

Francisco Maldonado went, and Juan de Guzman remained instead, Captain of his infantry. Of the Indians taken in Napetuca, the treasurer, Juan Gaytan, brought a youth with him, who stated that he did not belong to that country, but to one afar in the direction of the sun's rising, from which he had been a long time absent visiting other lands; that its name was Yupaha, and was governed by a woman, the town she lived in being of astonishing size, and many neighbouring lords her tributaries, some of whom gave her clothing, others gold in quantity. He showed how the metal was taken from the earth, melted, and refined, exactly as though he had seen it all done, or else the Devil had taught him how it was; so that they who knew aught of such matters declared it impossible that he could give that account without having been an eye-witness; and they who beheld the signs he made credited all that was understood as certain.

CHAPTER XIII

How the Governor went from Apalache in quest
of Yupaha, and what befell him.

On Wednesday, the third of March, in the year 1540, the Governor left Anhayca Apalache to seek Yupaha. He had ordered his men to go provided with maize for a march through sixty leagues of desert. The cavalry carried their grain on the horses, and the infantry theirs on the back; because the Indians they brought with them for service, being naked and in chains, had perished in great part during the winter. On the fourth day of the journey they arrived at a deep river, where a piragua was made; and, in consequence of the violence of the current, a cable of chains was extended from shore to shore, along which the boat passed, and the horses were drawn over, swimming thereto, by means of a windlass to the other side.

A day and a half afterwards, they arrived at a town by the name of Capachiqui, and on Friday,[1] the eleventh, the inhabitants were found to have gone off. The following day, five Christians, going in the rear of the camp to search for mortars, in which the natives beat maize, went to some houses surrounded by a thicket, where many Indians lurked as spies, an equal number of whom, separating from the rest, set upon our men, one of whom fled back, crying out to arms. When they who could first answer to the call reached the spot, they found one of the Christians killed, and the three others badly wounded, the Indians fleeing into a sheet of water, full of woods, into which the horses could not go. The Governor left Capachiqui, passing through a desert; and on Wednesday, the twenty-first[2] of the month, came to Toalli.

[1] The eleventh was Thursday, and it was on Thursday that they arrived at Capachiqui. *Cf.* Ranjel, Vol. II. p. 83. (B.)

[2] Wednesday was the twenty-fourth. The twenty-third was the day they arrived at Toalli, according to Ranjel. See Vol. II. p. 85. (B.)

The houses of this town were different from those behind, which were covered with dry grass; thenceforward they were roofed with cane, after the fashion of tile. They are kept very clean: some have their sides so made of clay as to look like tapia. Throughout the cold country every Indian has a winter house, plastered inside and out, with a very small door, which is closed at dark, and a fire being made within, it remains heated like an oven, so that clothing is not needed during the night-time. He has likewise a house for summer, and near it a kitchen, where fire is made and bread baked. Maize is kept in barbacoa, which is a house with wooden sides, like a room, raised aloft on four posts, and has a floor of cane. The difference between the houses of the masters, or principal men, and those of the common people is, besides being larger than the others, they have deep balconies on the front side, with cane seats, like benches; and about are many barbacoas, in which they bring together the tribute their people give them of maize, skins of deer, and blankets of the country. These are like shawls, some of them made from the inner bark of trees, and others of a grass resembling nettle, which, by treading out, becomes like flax. The women use them for covering, wearing one about the body from the waist downward, and another over the shoulder, with the right arm left free, after the manner of the Gypsies: the men wear but one, which they carry over the shoulder in the same way, the loins being covered with a bragueiro of deer-skin, after the fashion of the woollen breech-cloth that was once the custom of Spain. The skins are well dressed, the colour being given to them that is wished, and in such perfection, that, when of vermilion, they look like very fine red broadcloth; and when black, the sort in use for shoes, they are of the purest. The same hues are given to blankets.

The Governor left Toalli on the twenty-fourth day of March, and arrived on Thursday, in the evening, at a little stream where a small bridge was made, and the people passed to the opposite side. Benito Fernandes, a Portugues, fell off from it, and was drowned. So soon as the Governor had crossed, he found a town, a short way on, by the name of Achese, the people of which, having had no knowledge of the Christians, plunged into a river; nevertheless, some men and women were taken, among whom was found one who understood the youth, the guide to Yupaha, which rather confirmed what he stated, as they had come through regions speaking different languages, some of which he did not understand. By one of the Indians taken there, the Governor sent to call the Cacique from the farther side of the river, who, having come to him, thus spoke:

VERY HIGH, POWERFUL, AND GOOD MASTER:

The things that seldom happen bring astonishment. Think, then, what must be the effect on me and mine, the sight of you and your people, whom we have at no time seen, astride the fierce brutes, your horses, entering with such speed and fury into my country, that we had no tidings of your coming —things so altogether new, as to strike awe and terror to our hearts, which it was not nature to resist, so that we should receive you with the sobriety due to so kingly and famous a lord. Trusting to your greatness and personal qualities, I hope no fault will be found in me, and that I shall rather receive favours, of which one is that with my person, my country, and my vassals, you will do as with your own things; and another, that you tell me who you are, whence you come, whither you go, and what it is you seek, that I may the better serve you.

The Governor responded, that he greatly thanked him for his good-will, as much so as though he had given him a great treasure. He told him that he was the child of the Sun, coming from its abode, and that he was going about the country, seeking for the greatest prince there, and the richest province. The Cacique stated that farther on was a great lord, whose territory was called Ocute. He gave him a guide, who understood the language, to conduct him thither; and the Governor commanded his subjects to be released. A high cross, made of wood, was set up in the middle of the town-yard; and, as time did not allow more to be done, the Indians were instructed that it was put there to commemorate the suffering of Christ, who was God and man; that he had created the skies and the earth, and had suffered for the salvation of all, and therefore that they should revere that sign; and they showed by their manner that they would do so.

The Governor set out on the first day of April, and advanced through the country of the Chief, along up a river, the shores of which were very populous. On the fourth he went through the town of Altamaca, and on the tenth arrived at Ocute. The Cacique sent him a present, by two thousand Indians, of many conies and partridges, maize bread, many dogs, and two turkeys. On account of the scarcity of meat, the dogs were as much esteemed by the Christians as though they had been fat sheep. There was such want of salt also, that oftentimes, in many places, a sick man having nothing for his nourishment, and was wasting away to bone, of some ail that elsewhere might have found a remedy, when sinking under pure debility he would say: "Now, if I had but a slice of meat, or only a few lumps of salt, I should not thus die."

The Indians never lacked meat. With arrows they get abundance of deer, turkeys, conies, and other wild animals, being very skilful in killing game, which the Christians were not; and even if they had been, there was not the opportunity for it, they being on the march the greater part of their time; nor did they, besides, ever dare to straggle off. Such was the craving for meat, that when the six hundred men who followed Soto arrived at a town, and found there twenty or thirty dogs, he who could get sight of one and kill him, thought he had done no little; and he who proved himself so active, if his Captain knew of it, and he forgot to send him a quarter, would show his displeasure, and make him feel it in the watches, or in any matter of labour that came along, with which he could bear upon him.

On Monday, the twelfth of April, the Governor took his departure, the Cacique of Ocute giving him four hundred tamemes, the Indians that carry burdens. He passed through a town, the lord of which was called Cofaqui, and came to the province of another, named Patofa, who, being at peace with the Chief of Ocute and other neighbouring lords, had heard of the Governor for a long time, and desired to see him. He went to call on him, and made this speech:

POWERFUL LORD:

Not without reason, now, will I ask that some light mishap befall me, in return for so great good fortune, and deem my lot a happy one; since I have come to what I most wished in life, to behold and have the opportunity in some way to serve you. Thus the tongue casts the shadow of the thought; but I, nevertheless, am as unable to produce the perfect image of my feelings as to control the appearances of my contentment. By what circumstance has this your land, which I govern, deserved to be seen by one so superior and excellent that all on earth should obey and serve as prince. And those who here inhabit being so insignificant, how can they forget, in receiving this vast enjoyment, that, in the order of things, will follow upon it some great adversity? If we are held worthy of being yours, we can never be other than favoured, nor less than protected in whatsoever is reasonable and just; for they that fail of deserving either, with the name of men can only be considered brutes. From the depth of my heart, and with the respect due to such a chief, I make mine offer; and pray that, in return for so sincere good-will, you dispose of me, my country, and my vassals.

The Governor answered that his offers and good-will, shown in works, would greatly please him, and which he should ever bear in memory to honour and favour him as he would a brother. From this Province of Patofa, back to the first Cacique we found at peace, a distance of fifty leagues, the country is abundant, picturesque, and luxuriant, well watered, and having good river margins; thence to the harbour of Espiritu Santo, where we first arrived, the land of Florida, which may be three hundred leagues in length, a little more or less, is light, the greater part of it of pine-trees, and low, having many ponds; and in places are high and dense forest, into which the Indians that were hostile betook themselves, where they could not be found; nor could horses enter there, which, to the Christians, was the loss of the food they carried away, and made it troublesome to get guides.

CHAPTER XIIII

How the Governor left the Province of Patofa, marching into a Desert Country, where he, with his People, became exposed to great Peril and underwent severe Privation.

In the town of Patofa, the youth, whom the Governor brought with him for guide and interpreter, began to froth at the mouth, and threw himself on the ground as if he were possessed of the Devil. An exorcism being said over him, the fit went off. He stated that four days' journey from there, towards the sunrise, was the Province he spoke of: the Indians at Patofa said that they knew of no dwellings in that direction, but that towards the northwest there was a province called Coça, a plentiful country having very large towns. The Cacique told the Governor that if he desired to go thither he would give him a guide and Indians to carry burdens, and if he would go in the direction pointed out by the youth, he would furnish him with everything necessary for that also.

With words of love, and tendering each other services, they parted, the Governor receiving seven hundred tamemes. He took maize for the consumption of four days, and marched by a road that, gradually becoming less, on the sixth day it disappeared. Led by the youth, they forded two rivers, each the breadth of two shots of a crossbow, the water rising to the stirrups of the saddles, and passing in a current so powerful, that it became necessary for those on horseback to stand one before another, that they on foot, walking near, might cross along above them: then came to another of a more violent current, and larger, which was got over with more difficulty, the horses swimming for a lance's length at the coming out, into a pine-grove. The Governor menaced the youth, motioning that he would throw him to the dogs for having lied to him in saying that it was four days' journey, whereas they had travelled nine, each day of seven or eight leagues; and that the men and horses had become very thin, because of the sharp economy practised with the maize. The youth declared that he knew not where he was. Fortunately for him, at the time, there was not another whom Juan Ortez understood, or he would have been cast to the dogs.

The Governor, leaving the camp among the pine-trees, marched that day, with some cavalry and infantry, five or six leagues, looking for a path, and came back at night very cast down, not having found any sign of inhabitants. The next day there was a variety of opinion about the course proper to take, whether to return or do otherwise. The country through which they had come remained wasted and without maize; the grain they had so far brought with them was spent; the beasts, like the men, were become very lean; and it was held very doubtful whether relief was anywhere to be found: moreover, it was the opinion that they might be beaten by any Indians whatsoever who should venture to attack them, so that continuing thus, whether by hunger or in strife, they must inevitably be overcome. The Governor determined to send thence in all directions on horseback, in quest of habitations; and the next day he dispatched four captains to as many points, with eight of cavalry to each. They came back at night leading their beasts by the bridle, unable to carry their masters, or driven before them with sticks, having found no road, nor any sign of a settlement. He sent other four again the next day, with eight of cavalry apiece, men who could swim, that they might cross any ponds and rivers in the way, the horses being chosen of the best that were; Baltasar de Gallegos ascending by the river, Juan de Añasco going down it, Alfonso Romo and Juan Rodriguez Lobillo striking into the country.

The Governor had brought thirteen sows to Florida, which had increased to three hundred swine; and the maize having failed for three or four days, he ordered to be killed daily, for each man, half a pound of pork, on which small allowance, and some boiled herbs, the people with much difficulty lived. There being no food to give to the Indians of Patofa, they were dismissed, though they still wished to keep with the Christians in their extremity, and showed great regret at going back before leaving them in a peopled country. Juan de Añasco came in on Sunday, in the afternoon, bringing with him a woman and a youth he had taken, with the report that he had found a small town twelve or thirteen leagues off; at which the Governor and his people were as much delighted as though they had been raised from death to live.

On Monday, the twenty-sixth of April, the Governor set out for Aymay, a town to which the Christians gave the name of Socorro. At the foot of a tree, in the camp, they buried a paper, and in the bark, with a hatchet, they cut these words: " Dig here; at the root of this pine you will find a letter; " and this was so fixed that the Captains, who had gone in quest of an inhabited country, should learn what the Governor had done and the direction he had taken. There was no other road than the one Juan de Añasco had made moving along through the woods.

On Monday the Governor arrived at the town, with those the best mounted, all riding the hardest possible; some sleeping two leagues off, others three and four, each as he was able to travel and his strength held out. A barbacoa was found full of parched meal and some maize, which were distributed by allowance. Four Indians were taken, not one of whom would say any thing else than that he knew of no other town. The Governor ordered one of them to be burned; and thereupon another said, that two days' journey

from there was a province called Cutifachiqui.

On Wednesday the three Captains came
up: they had found the letter and followed
on after the rest. From the command of
Juan Rodriguez two men remained behind,
their horses having given out, for which the
Governor reprimanded him severely, and sent
him to bring them. While they should be
coming on he set out for Cutifachiqui, capturing three Indians in the road, who stated
that the mistress of that country had already
information of the Christians, and was waiting for them in a town. He sent to her by
one of them, offering his friendship and an-
nouncing his approach. Directly as the Governor arrived, four canoes came towards him,
in one of which was a kinswoman of the
Cacica, who, coming near, addressed him in
these words:

EXCELLENT LORD:

My sister sends me to salute you, and to say, that
the reason why she has not come in person is, that
she has thought to serve you better by remaining to
give orders on the other shore; and that, in a short
time, her canoes will all be here, in readiness to
conduct you thither, where you may take your repose
and be obeyed.

The Governor thanked her, and she returned to cross the river. After a little time

the Cacica came out of the town, seated in a
chair, which some principal men having borne
to the bank, she entered a canoe. Over the
stern was spread an awning, and in the bottom lay extended a mat where were two cushions, one above the other, upon which she sate;
and she was accompanied by her chief men, in
other canoes, with Indians. She approached
the spot where the Governor was, and, being
arrived, thus addressed him:

EXCELLENT LORD:

Be this coming to these your shores most happy.
My ability can in no way equal my wishes, nor my
services become the merits of so great a prince;
nevertheless, good wishes are to be valued more
than all the treasures of the earth without them.
With sincerest and purest good-will I tender you
my person, my lands, my people, and make you these
small gifts.

The Cacica presented much clothing of the
country, from the shawls and skins that came
in the other boats; and drawing from over
her head a large string of pearls, she threw
them about his neck, exchanging with him
many gracious words of friendship and courtesy. She directed that canoes should come
to the spot, whence the Governor and his
people passed to the opposite side of the river.
So soon as he was lodged in the town, a great
many turkeys were sent to him. The coun-

try was delightful and fertile, having good
interval lands upon the streams; the forest
was open, with abundance of walnut and
mulberry trees. The sea was stated to be
two days' travel. About the place, from half
a league to a league off, were large vacant
towns, grown up in grass, that appeared as if
no people had lived in them for a long time.
The Indians said that, two years before, there
had been a pest in the land, and the inhabitants
had moved away to other towns. In the
barbacoas were large quantities of clothing,
shawls of thread, made from the bark of
trees, and others of feathers, white, gray, vermilion, and yellow, rich and proper for winter.
There were also many well-dressed deer-skins,
of colours drawn over with designs, of which
had been made shoes, stockings, and hose.
The Cacica, observing that the Christians
valued pearls, told the Governor that, if he
should order some sepulchres that were in
the town to be searched, he would find many;
and if he chose to send to those that were in
the uninhabited towns, he might load all his
horses with them. They examined those in
the town, and found three hundred and fifty
pounds' weight of pearls, and figures of babies
and birds made of them.

The inhabitants are brown of skin, well
formed and proportioned. They are more

civilized than any people seen in all the territories of Florida, wearing clothes and shoes.
This country, according to what the Indians
stated, had been very populous. It appeared
that the youth who was the guide had heard
of it; and what was told him he declared to
have seen, and magnified such parts as he
chose, to suit his pleasure. He told the Governor that they had begun to enter upon the
country he had spoken to him about, which,
because of its appearance, with his being able
to understand the language of the people,
gained for him some credit. He wished to
become a Christian, and asked to be baptized,
which was done, he receiving the name of
Pedro; and the Governor commanded the
chain to be struck off that he had carried
until then.

In the town were found a dirk and beads
that had belonged to Christians, who, the
Indians said, had many years before been in
the port, distant two days' journey. He that
had been there was the Governor-licentiate
Ayllon, who came to conquer the land, and,
on arriving at the port, died, when there
followed divisions and murders among the
chief personages, in quarrels as to who should
command; and thence, without knowing any
thing of the country, they went back to
Spain.

To all it appeared well to make a settlement there, the point being a favourable one, to which could come all the ships from New Spain, Peru, Sancta Marta, and Tierra-Firme, going to Spain; because it is in the way thither, is·a good country, and one fit in which to raise supplies; but Soto, as it was his object to find another treasure like that of Atabalípa, lord of Peru, would not be content with good lands nor pearls, even though many of them were worth their weight in gold (and if the country were divided among Christians, more precious should those be the Indians would procure than these they have, being bored with heat, which causes them to lose their hue): so he answered them who urged him to make a settlement, that in all the country together there was not support for his troops a single month; that it was necessary to return to Ochus, where Maldonado was to wait; and should a richer country not be found, they could always return to that who would, and in their absence the Indians would plant their fields and be better provided with maize. The natives were asked if they had knowledge of any great lord farther on, to which they answered, that twelve days' travel thence was a province called Chiaha, subject to a chief of Coça.

The Governor then resolved at once to go

in quest of that country, and being an inflexible man, and dry of word, who, although he liked to know what the others all thought and had to say, after he once said a thing he did not like to be opposed, and as he ever acted as he thought best, all bent to his will; for though it seemed an error to leave that country, when another might have been found about it, on which all the people could have been sustained until the crops had been made and the grain gathered, there were none who would say a thing to him after it became known that he had made up his mind.

CHAPTER XV

How the Governor went from Cutifachiqui in quest of Coca, and what occurred to him on the Journey.

On the third day of May[1] the Governor set out from Cutifachiqui; and, it being discovered that the wish of the Cacica was to leave the Christians, if she could, giving them neither guides nor tamemes, because of the outrages committed upon the inhabitants, there never failing to be men of low degree among the many, who will put the lives of themselves and others in jeopardy for some mean inter-

[1] The date apparently should be the thirteenth. *Cf.* Ranjel, Vol. II. p. 102. (B.)

est, the Governor ordered that she should be placed under guard and took her with him. This treatment, which was not a proper return for the hospitable welcome he had received, makes true the adage, For well doing . . .; and thus she was carried away on foot with her female slaves.

This brought us service in all the places that were passed, she ordering the Indians to come and take the loads from town to town. We travelled through her territories a hundred leagues, in which, according to what we saw, she was greatly obeyed, whatsoever she ordered being performed with diligence and efficacy. Pedro, the guide, said she was not the suzeraine, but her niece, who had come to that town by her command to punish capitally some principal Indians who had seized upon the tribute; but to this no credit was given, because of the falsehoods in which he had been taken, though all was put up with, from the necessity of having some one whereby to understand what the Indians said.

In seven days the Governor arrived at the Province of Chelaque, the country poorest off for maize of any that was seen in Florida, where the inhabitants subsisted on the roots of plants that they dig in the wilds, and on the animals they destroy with their arrows. They are very domestic people, are slight of

form, and go naked. One lord brought the
Governor two deer-skins as a great gift.
Turkeys were abundant; in one town they
presented seven hundred, and in others brought
him what they had and could procure. He
was detained in going from this province to
that of Xualla five days, where they found
little grain, but remained two days, because
of the weariness of the men and the leanness
of the horses.

From Ocute to Cutifachiqui are one hundred and thirty leagues, of which eighty are
desert; from Cutifa to Xualla are two hundred and fifty of mountainous country; thence
to Guaxule, the way is over very rough and
lofty ridges.

One day while on this journey, the Cacica
of Cutifachi, whom the Governor brought
with him, as has been stated, to the end of
taking her to Guaxule, the farthest limit of
her territories, conducted by her slaves, she
left the road, with an excuse of going into a
thicket, where, deceiving them, she so concealed herself that for all their search she
could not be found. She took with her a cane
box, like a trunk, called petaca, full of un-
bored pearls, of which, those who had the most
knowledge of their value said they were very
precious. They were carried for her by one
of the women; and the Governor, not to give

offence, permitted it so, thinking that in Guaxule he would beg them of her when he should give her leave to depart; but she took them with her, going to Xualla, with three slaves who had fled from the camp. A horseman, named Alimamos, who remained behind, sick of a fever, wandering out of the way, got lost; and he laboured with the slaves to make them leave their evil design. Two of them did so, and came on with him to the camp. They overtook the Governor, after a journey of fifty leagues, in a province called Chiaha; and he reported that the Cacica remained in Xualla, with a slave of André de Vasconcelos, who would not come with him, and that it was very sure they lived together as man and wife, and were to go together to Cutifachiqui.

At the end of five days the Governor arrived at Guaxule. The Christians being seen to go after dogs, for their flesh, which the Indians do not eat, they gave them three hundred of those animals. Little maize was found there, or anywhere upon that route. The Governor sent a native with a message to the Cacique of Chiaha, begging that he would order some maize to be brought together at his town, that he might sojourn there some time. He left Guaxule, and after two days' travel arrived at Canasagua, where twenty

men came out from the town on the road, each
laden with a basket of mulberries. This fruit
is abundant and good, from Cutifachique to
this place, and thence onward in other provinces, as are the walnut and the *amiexa;* the
trees growing about over the country, without
planting or pruning, of the size and luxuriance
they would have were they cultivated in
orchards, by hoeing and irrigation. Leaving
Canasagua, he marched five days through a
desert.

Two leagues before coming to Chiaha,
fifteen men met the Governor, bearing loads
of maize, with word from the Cacique that he
waited for him, having twenty barbacoas full;
that, moreover, himself, his lands, and his
vassals, were subject to his orders. On the fifth
day of July [4] the Governor entered Chiaha.
The Cacique received him with great pleasure,
and, resigning to him his dwellings for his
residence, thus addressed him:

POWERFUL AND EXCELLENT MASTER:

Fortunate am I that you will make use of my
services. Nothing could happen that would give me
so great contentment, or which I should value more.
From Guaxule you sent to have maize for you in
readiness to last two months: you have in this town
twenty barbacoas full of the choicest and the best

[4] It should be June. See, below, p. 78, and *Cf.*
Ranjel, Vol. II. p. 107. (B.)

to be found in all this country. If the reception I give is not worthy of so great a prince, consider my youth, which will relieve me of blame, and receive my good-will, which, with true loyalty and pure, shall ever be shown in all things that concern your welfare.

The Governor answered him, that his gifts and his kindness pleased him greatly, and that he should ever consider him to be his brother.

There was abundance of lard in calabashes, drawn like olive oil, which the inhabitants said was the fat of bear. There was likewise found much oil of walnuts, which, like the lard, was clear and of good taste; and also a honey-comb, which the Christians had never seen before, nor saw afterwards, nor honey, nor bees, in all the country.

The town was isolated, between two arms of a river, and seated near one of them. Above it, at the distance of two crossbow-shot, the water divided, and united again a league below. The vale between, from side to side, was the width in places of a crossbow-shot, and in others of two. The branches were very wide, and both were fordable: along their shores were very rich meadow-lands, having many maize-fields.

As the Indians remained at home, no houses were taken save those of the Chief, in which the Governor lodged; the people lived out, wherever there happened to be shelter, each man having his tree. In this manner the army lay, the men out of order and far apart. The Governor passed it over, as the Indians were peaceful, and the weather very calm: the people would have suffered greatly had they been required to do differently. The horses arrived so worn out, that they could not bear their riders from weakness; for they had come all the way having only a little maize to live on, travelling, hungry and tired, even from beyond the desert of Ocute; so, as the greater part of them were unfit to be mounted, even in the necessary case of battle, they were turned out at night to graze, about a quarter of a league from the camp. The Christians were greatly exposed, so much so that if at that time the Indians had set upon them, they would have been in bad way to defend themselves.

The duration of the sojourn was thirty days, in which time, the soil being covered with verdure, the horses fattened. At the departure, in consequence of the importunity of some who wanted more than was in reason, the Governor asked thirty women of the Chief for slaves, who replied that he would confer with his principal men; when one night, before giving an answer, all went off from the town with their women and children. The next day, having made up his mind to go in search of them, the Cacique arrived, and, approaching, thus addressed him:

POWERFUL LORD:

Because of my shame, and out of fear of you, discovering that my subjects, contrary to my wishes, had chosen to absent themselves, I left without your permission; but, finding the error of my way, I have returned like a true vassal, to put myself in your power, that you may do with my person as shall seem best to you. My people will not obey me, nor do any thing that an uncle of mine does not command: he governs this country, in my place until I shall be of mature age. If you would pursue and punish them for disobedience, I will be your guide, since my fate at present forbids me doing more.

The Governor then, with thirty mounted men and as many footmen, went in search of the people. Passing by the towns of some of the chiefs who had gone off, he cut down and destroyed the great maize-fields; and going along up the stream where the natives were, on an islet, to which the calvary could not go, he sent word to them, by an Indian, that they should put away all their fears, and, returning to their abodes, give him tamemes, as had been done all the way along, since he did not wish to have women, finding how very dear they were to them. The Indians judged it well to come and make their excuses to him, so they all went back to the town.

A Cacique of Acoste, who came to see the Governor, after tendering his services, and they had exchanged compliments and proffers of friendship, was asked if he had any information of a rich land; he answered yes: that towards the north there was a province called Chisca, and that a forge was there for copper, or other metal of that colour, though brighter, having a much finer hue, and was to appearances much better, but was not so much used, for being softer; which was the statement that had been given in Cutifachiqui, where we had seen some chopping-knives that were said to have a mixture of gold. As the country on the way was thinly peopled, and it was said there were mountains over which the beasts could not go, the Governor would not march directly thither, but judged that, keeping in an inhabited territory the men and animals would be in better condition, while he would be more exactly informed of what there was, until he should turn to it through the ridges and a region which he could more easily travel. He sent two Christians to the country of Chisca, by Indians who spoke the language, that they might view it, and were told that he would await their return at Chiaha for what they should have to say.

CHAPTER XVI

How the Governor left Chiaha, and, having run a hazard of falling by the Hands of the Indians, at Acoste, escaped by his Address: what occurred to him on the Route, and how he came to Coca.

WHEN the Governor had determined to move from Chiaha towards Coste, he sent for the Cacique to come before him, and with kind words took his leave, receiving some slaves as a gift, which pleased him. In seven days the journey was concluded. On the second day of July, the camp being pitched among the trees, two crossbow-shot distant from the town, he went with eight men of his guard toward where the Cacique was, who received him evidently with great friendship. While they were conversing, some infantry went into the town after maize, and, not satisfied with what they got, they rummaged and searched the houses, taking what they would; at which conduct the owners began to rise and arm; some of them, with clubs in their hands, going at five or six men who had given offence, beat them to their satisfaction. The Governor, discovering that they were all bent upon some mischief, and himself among them with but few Christians about him, turned to escape

from the difficulty by a stratagem much against
his nature, clear and reliable as it was, and
the more unwillingly as it grieved him that
an Indian should presume, either with or
without cause, to offer any indignity to a
Christian: he seized a stave and took part
with the assailants against his own people,
which while it gave confidence, directly he
sent a message secretly to the camp, that armed
men should approach where he was; then
taking the Chief by the hand, speaking to him
with kind words, drew him with some principal men away from the town, out into an
open road in sight of the encampment, where
cautiously the Christians issued and by degrees
surrounded them. In this manner they were
conducted within the tents; and when near
his marquee the Governor ordered them to be
put under guard. He told them that they
could not go thence without giving him a
guide and Indians for carrying loads, nor until
the sick men had arrived whom he had ordered
to come down by the river in canoes from
Chiaha, and so likewise those he had sent to
the Province of Chisca. He feared that both
the one and the other had been killed by the
Indians. In three days they that went to
Chisca got back, and related that they had
been taken through a country so scant of
maize, and with such high mountains, that it

was impossible the army should march in that direction; and finding the distance was becoming long, and that they should be back late, upon consultation they agreed to return, coming from a poor little town where there was nothing of value, bringing a cow-hide as delicate as a calf-skin the people had given them, the hair being like the soft wool on the cross of the merino with the common sheep.

The Cacique having furnished the guide and tamemes, by permission of the Governor he went his way. The Christians left Coste the ninth day of July, and slept that night at Tali. The Cacique had come from the town to meet the Governor on the road, and made him this speech:

EXCELLENT GREAT PRINCE:

Worthy are you of being served and obeyed by all the princes of the world, for by the face can one judge far of the inner qualities. Who you are I knew, and also of your power, before your coming here. I wish not to draw attention to the lowliness in which I stand before you, to make my poor services acceptable and agreeable, since, where the strength fails, the will should instead be praised and taken. Hence, I dare to ask that you will only consider and attend to what you will command me to do here in your country.

The Governor answered, that his good-will and offer pleased him as much as though he had tendered him all the treasures of the earth: that he would always be treated by him as a true brother, favoured and esteemed. The Cacique ordered provision to be brought for two days' use, the time the Governor should be present; and on his departure, gave him the use of two men and four women, who were wanted to carry burdens.

They travelled six days, passing by many towns subject to the Cacique of Coça; and, as they entered those territories, numerous messengers came from him on the road every day to the Governor, some going, others coming, until they arrived at Coça, on Friday, the sixteenth of July. The Cacique came out to receive him at the distance of two crossbow-shot from the town, borne in a litter on the shoulders of his principal men, seated on a cushion, and covered with a mantle of marten-skins, of the size and shape of a woman's shawl: on his head he wore a diadem of plumes, and he was surrounded by many attendants playing upon flutes and singing. Coming to where the Governor was, he made his obeisance, and followed it by these words:

POWERFUL LORD, SUPERIOR TO EVERY OTHER OF THE
    EARTH:
Although I come but now to meet you, it is a long time since I have received you in my heart. That was done the first day I heard of you, with so great

desire to serve, please, and give you contentment, that this, which I express, is nothing in comparison with that which is within me. Of this you may be sure, that to have received the dominion of the world would not have interested me so greatly as the sight of you, nor would I have held it for so great a felicity. Do not look for me to offer you that which is your own—this person, these lands, these vassals. My only desire is to employ myself in commanding these people, that, with all diligence and befitting respect, they conduct you hence to the town in festivity of voices and with flutes, where you will be lodged and waited upon by me and them, where all I possess you will do with as with your own, and in thus doing you will confer favour.

The Governor gave him thanks, and with mutual satisfaction they walked on toward the place conferring, the Indians giving up their habitations by order of their Cacique, and in which the General and his men took lodging. In the barbacoas was a great quantity of maize and beans: the country, thickly settled in numerous and large towns, with fields between, extending from one to another, was pleasant, and had a rich soil with fair river margins. In the woods were many *ameixas,* as well those of Spain as of the country; and wild grapes on vines growing up into the trees, near the streams; likewise a kind that grew on low vines elsewhere, the berry being large and sweet, but, for want of hoeing and dressing, had large stones.

It was the practice to keep watch over the Caciques that none should absent themselves, they being taken along by the Governor until coming out of their territories; for by thus having them the inhabitants would await their arrival in the towns, give a guide, and men to carry the loads, who before leaving their country would have liberty to return to their homes, as sometimes would the tamemes, so soon as they came to the domain of any chief where others could be got. The people of Coça, seeing their lord was detained, took it amiss, and, going off, hid themselves in the scrub, as well those of the town of the Cacique as those of the towns of the principal men his vassals. The Governor dispatched four captains in as many directions to search for them: many men and women were taken who were put in chains. Seeing how much harm they received, and how little they gained by going off, they came in, declaring that they desired to serve in all that it were possible. Of the prisoners, some of the chiefs, whom the Cacique interceded for, were let go; of the rest, each one took away with him as slaves those he had in chains, none returning to their country save some whose fortune it was to escape, labouring diligently to file off their irons at night; or, while on the march, could slip out of the way, observing the carelessness of those who had them in charge, sometimes taking off with them in their chains the burdens and the clothing with which they were laded.

CHAPTER XVII

OF HOW THE GOVERNOR WENT FROM COCA TO TASTALUCA.

THE Governor rested in Coça twenty-five days. On Friday, the twentieth of August, he set out in quest of a province called Tastaluca, taking with him the Cacique of Coça. The first day he went through Tallimuchase, a great town without inhabitants, halting to sleep half a league beyond, near a river-bank. The following day he came to Ytaua, a town subject to Coça. . He was detained six days, because of a river near by that was then swollen: so soon as it could be crossed he took up his march, and went towards Ullibahali. Ten or twelve chiefs came to him on the road, from the Cacique of that province, tendering his service, bearing bows and arrows and wearing bunches of feathers.

The Governor having arrived at the town with a dozen cavalry and several of his guard, he left them at the distance of a crossbow-shot and entered the town. He found all the Indians with their weapons, and, according to their ways, it appeared to him in readiness for action: he understood afterwards that they had determined to wrest the Cacique of Coça from his power, should that chief have called on them. The place was enclosed, and near by ran a small stream. The fence, which was like that seen afterwards to other towns, was of large timber sunk deep and firmly into the earth, having many long poles the size of the arm, placed crosswise to nearly the height of a lance, with embrasures, and coated with mud inside and out, having loop-holes for archery. The Governor ordered all his men to enter the town. The Cacique, who at the moment was at a town on the opposite shore, was sent for, and he came at once. After some words between him and the Governor, proffering mutual service, he gave the tamemes that were requisite and thirty women as slaves. Mancano, a native of Salamanca, of noble ancestry, having strayed off in search of the grapes, which are good here, and plenty, was lost.

The Christians left, and that day they arrived to sleep at a town subject to the lord of Ullibahali, and the next day they came to pass the night at the town of Toasi, where the inhabitants gave the Governor thirty women and the tamemes that were wanted. The amount of travel usually performed was five or six leagues a day, passing through settled country; and when through desert, all the haste possible was made, to avoid the want of maize. From Toasi, passing through some towns subject to the lord of the Province of Tallise, he journeyed five days, and arrived at the town the eighteenth day of September.

Tallise was large, situated by the side of a great river, other towns and many fields of maize being on the opposite shore, the country on both sides having the greatest abundance of grain. The inhabitants had gone off. The Governor sent to call the Cacique, who, having arrived, after an interchange of kind words and good promises, lent him forty men. A chief came to the Governor in behalf of the Cacique of Tastaluca, and made the following address:

VERY POWERFUL, VIRTUOUS, AND ESTEEMED LORD:

The grand Cacique of Tastaluca, my master, sends me to salute you. He bids me say, that he is told how all, not without reason, are led captive by your perfections and power; that wheresoever lies your path you receive gifts and obedience, which he knows are all your due; and that he longs to see you as much as he could desire for the continuance of life. Thus, he sends me to offer you his person, his lands, his subjects; to say, that wheresoever it shall please you to go through his territories, you will find service and obedience, friendship and peace. In requital of this wish to serve you, he asks that you so far favour him as to say when you will come; for that the sooner you do so, the greater will be the obligation, and to him the earlier pleasure.

The Governor received and parted with the messenger graciously, giving him beads (which by the Indians are not much esteemed), and other articles, that he should take them to his lord. He dismissed the Cacique of Coça, that he might return to his country: he of Tallise gave him the tamemes that were needed; and, having sojourned twenty days, the Governor set out for Tastaluca. He slept the night at a large town called Casiste, and the next day, passing through another, arrived at a village in the Province of Tastaluca; and the following night he rested in a wood, two leagues from the town where the Cacique resided, and where he was then present. He sent the Field-Marshal, Luis de Moscoso, with fifteen cavalry, to inform him of his approach.

The Cacique was at home, in a piazza. Before his dwelling, on a high place, was spread a mat for him, upon which two cushions were placed, one above another, to which he went and sat down, his men placing themselves around, some way removed, so that an open circle was formed about him, the Indians of the highest rank being nearest to his person. One of them shaded him from the sun with a circular umbrella, spread wide, the size of a target, with a small stem, and having deer-skin extended over cross-sticks, quartered with red and white, which at a distance made it look of taffeta, the colours were so very perfect. It formed the standard of the Chief, which he carried into battle. His appearance was full of dignity: he was tall of person, muscular, lean, and symmetrical. He was the suzerain of many territories, and of a numerous people, being equally feared by his vassals and the neighbouring nations. The Field-Marshal, after he had spoken to him, advanced with his company, their steeds leaping from side to side, and at times towards the Chief, when he, with great gravity, and seemingly with indifference, now and then would raise his eyes, and look on as in contempt.

The Governor approached him, but he made no movement to rise; he took him by the hand, and they went together to seat themselves on the bench that was in the piazza. The Cacique addressed him these words:

POWERFUL CHIEF:
Your lordship is very welcome. With the sight of you I receive as great pleasure and comfort as though you were an own brother whom I dearly loved. It is idle to use many words here, as it is not well to speak at length where a few may suffice. The greater the will the more estimable the deed; and acts are the living witnesses of truth. You shall learn how strong and positive is my will, and how disinterested my inclination to serve you. The gifts

you did me the favour to send I esteem in all
their value, but most because they were yours. See
in what you will command me.

The Governor satisfied the Chief with a
few brief words of kindness. On leaving he
determined, for certain reasons, to take him
along. The second day on the road he came
to a town called Piache: a great river ran
near, and the Governor asked for canoes. The
Indians said they had none, but that they
could have rafts of cane and dried wood,
whereon they might readily enough go over,
which they diligently set about making, and
soon completed. They managed them; and
the water being calm, the Governor and his
men easily crossed.

From the port of Espiritu Santo to Palache,
a march of about a hundred leagues, the
course was west; from Apalache to Cutifachiqui, which may be four hundred and thirty
leagues, it was northeast; from thence to
Xualla, two hundred and fifty leagues, it was
towards the north; and thence to Tastaluca,
which may be some other two hundred and
fifty leagues, one hundred and ninety of them
were toward the west, going to the Province
of Coça, and the sixty southwardly, in going
thence to Tastaluca.

After crossing the river of Piache, a Christian having gone to look after a woman gotten

away from him, he had been either captured
or killed by the natives, and the Governor
pressed the Chief to tell what had been done;
threatening, that should the man not appear,
he would never release him. The Cacique
sent an Indian thence to Mauilla, the town of
a chief, his vassal, whither they were going,
stating that he sent to give him notice that he
should have provisions in readiness and Indians for loads; but which, as afterwards appeared, was a message for him to get together
there all the warriors in his country.

The Governor marched three days, the last
one of them continually through an inhabited
region, arriving on Monday, the eighteenth
day of October, at Mauilla. He rode forward in the vanguard, with fifteen cavalry
and thirty infantry, when a Christian he had
sent with a message to the Cacique, three or
four days before, with orders not to be gone
long, and to discover the temper of the Indians,
came out from the town and reported that
they appeared to him to be making preparation; for that while he was present many
weapons were brought, and many people came
into the town, and work had gone on rapidly
to strengthen the palisade. Luis de Moscoso
said that, since the Indians were so evil disposed, it would be better to stop in the woods;
to which the Governor answered, that he was

impatient of sleeping out, and that he would
lodge in the town.

Arriving near, the Chief came out to receive him, with many Indians singing and
playing on flutes, and after tendering his
services, gave him three cloaks of marten-
skins. The Governor entered the town with
the Caciques, seven or eight men of his guard,
and three or four cavalry, who had dismounted
to accompany them; and they seated themselves in a piazza. The Cacique of Tastaluca asked the Governor to allow him to remain there, and not to weary him any more
with walking; but, finding that was not to be
permitted, he changed his plan, and, under
pretext of speaking with some of the chiefs, he
got up from where he sate, by the side of the
Governor, and entered a house where were
many Indians with their bows and arrows. The
Governor, finding that he did not return,
called to him; to which the Cacique answered
that he would not come out, nor would he
leave that town; that if the Governor wished
to go in peace, he should quit at once, and not
persist in carrying him away by force from
his country and its dependencies.

CHAPTER XVIII

How the Indians rose upon the Governor, and what followed upon that rising.

THE Governor, in view of the determination and furious answer of the Cacique, thought to soothe him with soft words; to which he made no answer, but, with great haughtiness and contempt, withdrew to where Soto could not see nor speak to him. The Governor, that he might send word to the Cacique for him to remain in the country at his will, and to be pleased to give him a guide, and persons to carry burdens, that he might see if he could pacify him with gentle words, called to a chief who was passing by. The Indian replied, loftily, that he would not listen to him. Baltasar de Gallegos, who was near, seized him by the cloak of marten-skins that he had on, drew it off over his head, and left it in his hands; whereupon, the Indians all beginning to rise, he gave him a stroke with a cutlass, that laid open his back, when they, with loud yells, came out of the houses, discharging their bows.

The Governor, discovering that if he remained there they could not escape, and if he should order his men, who were outside of the town, to come in, the horses might be

killed by the Indians from the houses and great
injury done, he ran out; but before he could
get away he fell two or three times, and was
helped to rise by those with him. He and
they were all badly wounded: within the
town five Christians were instantly killed.
Coming forth, he called out to all his men to
get farther off, because there was much harm
doing from the palisade. The natives discovering that the Christians were retiring,
and some, if not the greater number, at more
than a walk, the Indians followed with great
boldness, shooting at them, or striking down
such as they could overtake. Those in chains
having set down their burdens near the fence
while the Christians were retiring, the people
of Mauilla lifted the loads on to their backs,
and, bringing them into the town, took off
their irons, putting bows and arms in their
hands, with which to fight. Thus did the
foe come into possession of all the clothing,
pearls, and whatsoever else the Christians had
beside, which was what their Indians carried.
Since the natives had been at peace to that
place, some of us, putting our arms in the
luggage, went without any; and two, who
were in the town, had their swords and hal-
berds taken from them, and put to use.

The Governor, presently as he found himself in the field, called for a horse, and, with

some followers, returned and lanced two or three of the Indians; the rest, going back into the town, shot arrows from the palisade. Those who would venture on their nimbleness came out a stone's throw from behind it, to fight, retiring from time to time, when they were set upon.

At the time of the affray there was a friar, a clergyman, a servant of the Governor, and a female slave in the town, who, having no time in which to get away, took to a house, and there remained until after the Indians became masters of the place. They closed the entrance with a lattice door; and there being a sword among them, which the servant had, he put himself behind the door, striking at the Indians that would have come in; while, on the other side, stood the friar and the priest, each with a club in hand, to strike down the first that should enter. The Indians, finding that they could not get in by the door, began to unroof the house: at this moment the cavalry were all arrived at Mauilla, with the infantry that had been on the march, when a difference of opinion arose as to whether the Indians should be attacked, in order to enter the town; for the result was held doubtful, but finally it was concluded to make the assault.

CHAPTER XIX

How the Governor sent his Men in order
of Battle and entered the town of
Mauilla.

So soon as the advance and the rear of the
force were come up, the Governor commanded
that all the best armed should dismount, of
which he made four squadrons of footmen.
The Indians, observing how he was going on
arranging his men, urged the Cacique to
leave, telling him, as was afterwards made
known by some women who were taken in
the town, that as he was but one man, and
could fight but as one only, there being many
chiefs present very skilful and experienced in
matters of war, any one of whom was able to
command the rest, and as things in war were
so subject to fortune, that it was never certain which side would overcome the other,
they wished him to put his person in safety;
for if they should conclude their lives there,
on which they had resolved rather than sur-
render, he would remain to govern the land:
but for all that they said, he did not wish to
go, until, from being continually urged, with
fifteen or twenty of his own people he went
out of the town, taking with him a scarlet
cloak and other articles of the Christians'

clothing, being whatever he could carry and that seemed best to him.

The Governor, informed that the Indians were leaving the town, commanded the cavalry to surround it; and into each squadron of foot he put a soldier, with a brand, to set fire to the houses, that the Indians might have no shelter. His men being placed in full concert, he ordered an arquebuse to be shot off: at the signal the four squadrons, at their proper points, commenced a furious onset, and, both sides severely suffering, the Christians entered the town. The friar, the priest, and the rest who were with them in the house, were all saved, though at the cost of the lives of two brave and very able men who went thither to their rescue. The Indians fought with so great spirit that they many times drove our people back out of the town. The struggle lasted so long that many Christians, weary and very thirsty, went to drink at a pond near by, tinged with the blood of the killed, and returned to the combat. The Governor, witnessing this, with those who followed him in the returning charge of the footmen, entered the town on horseback, which gave opportunity to fire the dwellings; then breaking in upon the Indians and beating them down, they fled out of the place, the cavalry and infantry driving them back through the gates, where, losing the hope of escape, they fought valiantly; and the Christians getting among them with cutlasses, they found themselves met on all sides by their strokes, when many, dashing headlong into the flaming houses, were smothered, and, heaped one upon another, burned to death.

They who perished there were in all two thousand five hundred, a few more or less: of the Christians there fell eighteen, among whom was Don Carlos, brother-in-law of the Governor; one Juan de Gamez, a nephew; Men, Rodriguez, a Portugues; and Juan Vazquez, of Villanueva de Barcarota, men of condition and courage; the rest were infantry. Of the living, one hundred and fifty Christians had received seven hundred wounds from the arrow; and God was pleased that they should be healed in little time of very dangerous injuries. Twelve horses died, and seventy were hurt. The clothing the Christians carried with them, the ornaments for saying mass, and the pearls, were all burned there; they having set the fire themselves, because they considered the loss less than the injury they might receive of the Indians from within the houses, where they had brought the things together.

The Governor learning in Mauilla that Francisco Maldonado was waiting for him in

the port of Ochuse, six days' travel distant,
he caused Juan Ortiz to keep the news secret,
that he might not be interrupted in his purpose; because the pearls he wished to send to
Cuba for show, that their fame might raise
the desire of coming to Florida, had been
lost, and he feared that, hearing of him without seeing either gold or silver, or other thing
of value from that land, it would come to have
such reputation that no one would be found
to go there when men should be wanted: so
he determined to send no news of himself
until he should have discovered a rich country.

CHAPTER XX

How the Governor set out from Mauilla to go to Chicaça, and what befell him.

From the time the Governor arrived in
Florida until he went from Mauilla, there
died one hundred and two Christians, some
of sickness, others by the hand of the Indians.
Because of the wounded, he stopped in that
place twenty-eight days, all the time remaining out in the fields. The country was a rich
soil, and well inhabited: some towns were very
large, and were picketed about. The people
were numerous everywhere; the dwellings
standing a crossbow-shot or two apart.

On Sunday, the eighteenth of November,[1] the sick being found to be getting on well, the Governor left Mauilla, taking with him a supply of maize for two days. He marched five days through a wilderness, arriving in a province called Pafallaya, at the town Taliepataua; and thence he went to another, named Cabusto, near which was a large river, whence the Indians on the farther bank shouted to the Christians that they would kill them should they come over there. He ordered the building of a piragua within the town, that the natives might have no knowledge of it; which being finished in four days, and ready, he directed it to be taken on sleds half a league up stream, and in the morning thirty men entered it, well armed. The Indians discovering what was going on, they who were nearest went to oppose the landing, and did the best they could; but the Christians drawing near, and the piragua being about to reach the shore, they fled into some cane-brakes. The men on horses went up the river to secure a landing-place, to which the Governor passed over, with the others that remained. Some of the towns were well stored with maize and beans.

[1] The eighteenth of November in 1540 was Thursday. It was on Sunday, November 14, that De Soto left Mauilla. *Cf.* Ranjel, Vol. II. p. 128. (B.)

Thence towards Chicaça the Governor marched five days through a desert, and arrived at a river, on the farther side of which were Indians, who wished to arrest his passage. In two days another piragua was made, and when ready he sent an Indian in it to the Cacique, to say, that if he wished his friendship he should quietly wait for him; but they killed the messenger before his eyes, and with loud yells departed. He crossed the river the seventeenth of December, and arrived the same day at Chicaça, a small town of twenty houses. There the people underwent severe cold, for it was already winter, and snow fell: the greater number were then lying in the fields, it being before they had time to put up habitations. The land was thickly inhabited, the people living about over it as they do in Mauilla; and as it was fertile, the greater part being under cultivation, there was plenty of maize. So much grain was brought together as was needed for getting through with the season.

Some Indians were taken, among whom was one the Cacique greatly esteemed. The Governor sent an Indian to the Cacique to say, that he desired to see him and have his friendship. He came, and offered him the services of his person, territories, and subjects: he said that he would cause two chiefs to visit him in peace. In a few days he returned with them, they bringing their Indians. They presented the Governor one hundred and fifty conies, with clothing of the country, such as shawls and skins. The name of the one was Alimamu, of the other Niculasa.

The Cacique of Chicaça came to visit him many times: on some occasions he was sent for, and a horse taken, on which to bring and carry him back. He made complaint that a vassal of his had risen against him, withholding tribute; and he asked for assistance, desiring to seek him in his territory, and give him the chastisement he deserved. The whole was found to be feigned, to the end that, while the Governor should be absent with him, and the force divided, they would attack the parts separately—some the one under him, others the other, that remained in Chicaça. He went to the town where he lived, and came back with two hundred Indians, bearing bows and arrows.

The Governor, taking thirty cavalry and eighty infantry, marched to Saquechuma, the Province of the Chief whom the Cacique said had rebelled. The town was untenanted, and the Indians, for greater dissimulation, set fire to it; but the people with the Governor being very careful and vigilant, as were also those that had been left in Chicaça, no enemy dared to fall upon them. The Governor invited the caciques and some chiefs to dine with him, giving them pork to eat, which they so relished, although not used to it, that every night Indians would come up to some houses where the hogs slept, a crossbow-shot off from the camp, to kill and carry away what they could of them. Three were taken in the act: two the Governor commanded to be slain with arrows, and the remaining one, his hands having first been cut off, was sent to the Cacique, who appeared grieved that they had given offence, and glad that they were punished.

This Chief was half a league from where the Christians were, in an open country, whither wandered off four of the cavalry: Francisco Osorio, Reynoso, a servant of the Marquis of Astorga, and two servants of the Governor,—the one Ribera, his page, the other Fuentes, his chamberlain. They took some skins and shawls from the Indians, who made great outcry in consequence, and abandoned their houses. When the Governor heard of it, he ordered them to be apprehended, and condemned Osorio and Fuentes to death, as principals, and all of them to lose their goods. The friars, the priests, and other principal personages solicited him to let Osorio

live, and moderate the sentence; but he would
do so for no one. When about ordering them
to be taken to the town-yard to be beheaded,
some Indians arrived, sent by the Chief to
complain of them. Juan Ortiz, at the en-
treaty of Baltasar de Gallegos and others,
changed their words, telling the Governor, as
from the Cacique, that he had understood those
Christians had been arrested on his account;
that they were in no fault, having offended
him in nothing, and that if he would do him
a favour, to let them go free: then Ortiz said
to the Indians, that the Governor had the
persons in custody, and would visit them
with such punishment as should be an example
to the rest. The prisoners were ordered to be
released.

So soon as March had come, the Governor,
having determined to leave Chicaça, asked two
hundred tamemes of the Cacique, who told
him that he would confer with his chiefs.
Tuesday, the eighth, he went where the Cacique was, to ask for the carriers, and was told
that he would send them the next day. When
the Governor saw the Chief, he said to Luis
de Moscoso that the Indians did not appear
right to him; that a very careful watch should
be kept that night, to which the Field Marshal
paid little attention. At four o'clock in the
morning the Indians fell upon them in four

squadrons, from as many quarters, and directly as they were discovered, they beat a drum. With loud shouting, they came in such haste, that they entered the camp at the same moment with some scouts that had been out; of which, by the time those in the town were aware, half the houses were in flames. That night it had been the turn of three horsemen to be of the watch,—two of them men of low degree, the least value of any in the camp, and the third a nephew of the Governor, who had been deemed a brave man until now, when he showed himself as great a coward as either of the others; for they all fled, and the Indians, finding no resistance, came up and set fire to the place. They waited outside of the town for the Christians, behind the gates, as they should come out of the doors, having had no opportunity to put on their arms; and as they ran in all directions, bewildered by the noise, blinded by the smoke and the brightness of the flame, knowing not whither they were going, or were able to find their arms, or put saddles on their steeds, they saw not the Indians who shot arrows at them. Those of the horses that could break their halters got away, and many were burned to death in the stalls.

The confusion and rout were so great that each man fled by the way that first opened to

him, there being none to oppose the Indians:
but God, who chastiseth his own as he
pleaseth, and in the greatest wants and perils
hath them in his hand, shut the eyes of the
Indians, so that they could not discern what
they had done, and believed that the beasts
running about loose were the cavalry gathering to fall upon them. The Governor, with
a soldier named Tápia, alone got mounted,
and, charging upon the Indians, he struck
down the first of them he met with a blow
of the lance, but went over with the saddle,
because in the haste it had not been tightly
drawn, and he fell. The men on foot, running to a thicket outside of the town, came
together there: the Indians imagining, as it
was dark, that the horses were cavalry coming upon them, as has been stated, they
fled, leaving only one dead, which was he the
Governor smote.

The town lay in cinders. A woman, with
her husband, having left a house, went back
to get some pearls that had remained there;
and when she would have come out again the
fire had reached the door, and she could not,
neither could her husband assist her, so she was
consumed. Three Christians came out of the
fire in so bad plight, that one of them died
in three days from that time, and the two
others for a long while were carried in their

pallets, on poles borne on the shoulders of
Indians, for otherwise they could not have got
along. There died in this affair eleven Christians, and fifty horses. One hundred of the
swine remained, four hundred having been
destroyed, from the conflagration of Mauilla.

If, by good luck, any one had been able to
save a garment until then, it was there destroyed. Many remained naked, not having
had time to catch up their skin dresses. In
that place they suffered greatly from cold,
the only relief being in large fires, and they
passed the night long in turning, without the
power to sleep; for as one side of a man would
warm, the other would freeze. Some con-
trived mats of dried grass sewed together, one
to be placed below, and the other above them:
many who laughed at this expedient were
afterwards compelled to do the like. The
Christians were left so broken up, that what
with the want of the saddles and arms which
had been destroyed, had the Indians returned
the second night, they might, with little
effort, have been overpowered. They removed
from that town to the one where the Cacique
was accustomed to live, because it was in the
open field. In eight days' time they had constructed many saddles from the ash, and likewise lances, as good as those made in Biscay.

CHAPTER XXI

How the Indians returned to attack the Christians, and how the Governor went to Alimamu, and they tarried to give him Battle
in the Way.

On Wednesday, the fifteenth day of
March,[1] in the year 1541, eight days having
passed since the Governor had been living
on a plain, half a league from the place
where he wintered, after he had set up a forge,
and tempered the swords which in Chicaça
had been burned, and already had made many
targets, saddles, and lances, at four o'clock
in the morning, while it was still dark,
there came many Indians, formed in three
squadrons, each from a different direction, to
attack the camp, when those who watched beat
to arms. In all haste he drew up his men in
three squadrons also, and leaving some for the
defence of the camp, he went out to meet
them. The Indians were overthrown and put
to flight. The ground was plain, and in a
condition advantageous to the Christians. It
was now daybreak; and but for some disorder,
thirty or forty more enemies might have been

[1] The fifteenth of March was Tuesday in 1541.
It was on Tuesday, March fifteenth, that this attack
occurred. *Cf.* Ranjel, Vol. II. p. 135. (B.)

slain. It was caused by a friar raising great shouts in the camp, without any reason, crying, "To the camp! To the camp!" In consequence the Governor and the rest went thither, and the Indians had time to get away in safety.

From some prisoners taken, the Governor informed himself of the region in advance. On the twenty-fifth day of April he left Chicaça and went to sleep at a small town called Alimamu. Very little maize was found; and as it became necessary to attempt thence to pass a desert, seven days' journey in extent, the next day the Governor ordered that three captains, each with cavalry and foot, should take a different direction, to get provision for the way. Juan de Añasco, the Comptroller, went with fifteen horse and forty foot on the course the Governor would have to march, and found a staked fort where the Indians were awaiting them. Many were armed, walking upon it, with their bodies, legs, and arms painted and ochred, red, black, white, yellow, and vermilion in stripes, so that they appeared to have on stockings and doublet. Some wore feathers, and others horns on the head, the face blackened, and the eyes encircled with vermilion, to heighten their fierce aspect. So soon as they saw the Christians draw nigh they beat drums, and,

with loud yells, in great fury came forth to
meet them. As to Juan de Añasco and others
it appeared well to avoid them, and to inform the Governor, they retired, over an
even ground in sight, the distance of a crossbow-shot from the enclosure, the footmen, the
crossbow-men, and targeteers putting themselves before those on horseback, that the
beasts might not be wounded by the Indians,
who came forth by sevens and eights to discharge their bows at them and retire. In
sight of the Christians they made a fire, and,
taking an Indian by the head and feet, pretended to give him many blows on the head
and cast him into the flames, signifying in this
way what they would do with the Christians.

A message being sent with three of the
cavalry to the Governor, informing him of
this, he came directly. It was his opinion that
they should be driven from the place. He
said that if this was not done they would be
emboldened to make an attack at some other
time, when they might do him more harm:
those on horseback were commanded to dismount, and, being set in four squadrons, at
the signal charged the Indians. They resisted
until the Christians came up to the stakes;
then, seeing that they could not defend themselves, they fled through that part near which
passed a stream, sending back some arrows

from the other bank; and because, at the moment, no place was found where the horses might ford, they had time to make their escape. Three Indians were killed and many Christians wounded, of whom, after a few days, fifteen died on the march. Every one thought the Governor committed a great fault in not sending to examine the state of the ground on the opposite shore, and discover the crossing-place before making the attack; because, with the hope the Indians had of escaping unseen in that direction, they fought until they were broken; and it was the cause of their holding out so long to assail the Christians, as they could, with safety to themselves.

CHAPTER XXII

How the Governor went from Quizquiz, and thence to the River Grande.

THREE days having gone by since some maize had been sought after, and but little found in comparison with the great want there was of it, the Governor became obliged to move at once, nothwithstanding the wounded had need of repose, to where there should be abundance. He accordingly set out for Quizquiz, and marched seven days through a wilderness, having many pondy places, with thick forests, fordable, however, on horseback, all to some basins or lakes that were swum.[1] He arrived at a town of Quizquiz without being descried, and seized all the people before they could come out of their houses. Among them was the mother of the Cacique; and the Governor sent word to him, by one of the captives, to come and receive her, with the rest he had taken. The answer he returned was, that if his lordship would order them to be loosed and sent, he would come to visit and do him service.

The Governor, since his men arrived weary, and likewise weak, for want of maize, and the horses were also lean, determined to yield to the requirement and try to have peace; so the mother and the rest were ordered to be set free, and with words of kindness were dismissed. The next day, while he was hoping to see the Chief, many Indians came, with bows and arrows, to set upon the Christians, when he commanded that all the armed horsemen should be mounted and in readiness. Finding them prepared, the Indians stopped at the distance of a crossbow-shot from where the Governor was, near a river-bank, where, after remaining quietly half an hour, six chiefs arrived at the camp, stating that they had

[1] This clause should read, "all passable, however, on horseback, except some basins," etc. (B.)

come to find out what people it might be; for
that they had knowledge from their ancestors
that they were to be subdued by a white race;
they consequently desired to return to the
Cacique, to tell him that he should come
presently to obey and serve the Governor.
After presenting six or seven skins and shawls
brought with them, they took their leave, and
returned with the others who were waiting
for them by the shore. The Cacique came
not, nor sent another message.

There was little maize in the place, and
the Governor moved to another town, half a
league from the great river,[2] where it was
found in sufficiency. He went to look at the
river, and saw that near it there was much
timber of which piraguas might be made, and
a good situation in which the camp might be
placed. He directly moved, built houses, and
settled on a plain a crossbow-shot from the
water, bringing together there all the maize
of the towns behind, that at once they might
go to work and cut down trees for sawing out
planks to build barges. The Indians soon
came from up the stream, jumped on shore, and
told the Governor that they were the vassals
of a great lord, named Aquixo, who was the
suzerain of many towns and people on the
other shore; and they made known from him,

[2] The Mississippi. (B.)

that he would come the day after, with all
his people, to hear what his lordship would
command him.

The next day the Cacique arrived, with two
hundred canoes filled with men, having
weapons. They were painted with ochre,
wearing great bunches of white and other
plumes of many colours, having feathered
shields in their hands, with which they sheltered the oarsmen on either side, the warriors
standing erect from bow to stern, holding bows
and arrows. The barge in which the Cacique
came had an awning at the poop, under which
he sate; and the like had the barges of the
other chiefs: and there, from under the
canopy, where the chief man was, the course
was directed and orders issued to the rest.
All came down together, and arrived within
a stone's cast of the ravine, whence the
Cacique said to the Governor, who was walking along the river-bank, with others who
bore him company, that he had come to visit,
serve, and obey him; for he had heard that
he was the greatest of lords, the most powerful on all the earth, and that he must see
what he would have him do. The Governor
expressed his pleasure, and besought him to
land, that they might the better confer;
but the Chief gave no reply, ordering three
barges to draw near, wherein was great quan-

tity of fish, and loaves like bricks, made of the pulp of *ameixas,* which Soto receiving, gave him thanks and again entreated him to land.

Making the gift had been a pretext, to discover if any harm might be done; but, finding the Governor and his people on their guard, the Cacique began to draw off from the shore, when the crossbow-men who were in readiness, with loud cries shot at the Indians, and struck down five or six of them. They retired with great order, not one leaving the oar, even though the one next to him might have fallen, and covering themselves, they withdrew. Afterwards they came many times and landed; when approached, they would go back to their barges. These were fine-looking men, very large and well formed; and what with the awnings, the plumes, and the shields, the pennons, and the number of people in the fleet, it appeared like a famous armada of galleys.

During the thirty days that were passed there, four piraguas were built, into three of which, one morning, three hours before daybreak, the Governor ordered twelve cavalry to enter, four in each, men in whom he had confidence that they would gain the land, notwithstanding the Indians, and secure the passage, or die: he also sent some crossbow-men of foot with them, and in the other piragua, oarsmen, to take them to the opposite shore. He ordered Juan de Guzman to cross with the infantry, of which he had remained Captain in the place of Francisco Maldonado; and because the current was stiff, they went up along the side of the river a quarter of a league, and in passing over they were carried down, so as to land opposite the camp; but, before arriving there, at twice the distance of a stone's cast, the horsemen rode out from the piraguas to an open area of hard and even ground, where they all reached without accident.

So soon as they had come to shore the piraguas returned; and when the sun was up two hours high, the people had all got over. The distance was near half a league: a man standing on the shore could not be told, whether he were a man or something else, from the other side. The stream was swift, and very deep; the water, always flowing turbidly, brought along from above many trees and much timber, driven onward by its force. There were many fish of several sorts, the greater part differing from those of the fresh waters of Spain, as will b.. told hereafter.

CHAPTER XXIII

How the Governor went from Aquixo to Casqui, and thence to Pacaha; and how this Country differs from the other.

THE Rio Grande being crossed, the Governor marched a league and a half, to a large town of Aquixo, which was abandoned before his arrival. Over a plain thirty Indians were seen to draw nigh, sent by the Cacique, to discover what the Christians intended to do, but who fled directly as they saw them. The cavalry pursued, killed ten, and captured fifteen. As the town toward which the Governor marched was near the river, he sent a captain, with the force he thought sufficient, to take the piraguas up the stream. These, as they frequently wound about through the country, having to go round the bays that swell out of the river, the Indians had opportunity to attack those in the piraguas, placing them in great peril, being shot at with bows from the ravines, while they dared not leave the shore, because of the swiftness of the current; so that, as soon as the Governor got to the town, he directly sent crossbow-men to them down the stream, for their protection. When the piraguas arrived, he ordered them to be taken to pieces, and the spikes kept for making others, when they should be needed.

The Governor slept at the town one night, and the day following he went in quest of a province called Pacaha, which he had been informed was nigh Chisca, where the Indians said there was gold. He passed through large towns in Aquixo, which the people had left for fear of the Christians. From some Indians that were taken, he heard that three days' journey thence resided a great Cacique, called Casqui. He came to a small river, over which a bridge was made, whereby he crossed. All that day, until sunset, he marched through water, in places coming to the knees; in others, as high as the waist. They were greatly rejoiced on reaching the dry land; because it had appeared to them that they should travel about, lost, all night in the water. At midday they came to the first town of Casqui, where they found the Indians off their guard, never having heard of them. Many men and women were taken, much clothing, blankets, and skins; such they likewise took in another town in sight of the first, half a league off in the field, whither the horsemen had run.

This land is higher, drier, and more level than any other along the river that had been seen until then. In the fields were many walnut-trees, bearing tender-shelled nuts in the shape of acorns, many being found stored in the houses. The tree did not differ in any thing from that of Spain, nor from the one seen before, except the leaf was smaller. There were many mulberry-trees, and trees of *ameixas,* having fruit of vermilion hue, like one of Spain, while others were gray, differing, but far better. All the trees, the year round, were as green as if they stood in orchards, and the woods were open.

The Governor marched two days through the country of Casqui, before coming to the town where the Cacique was, the greater part of the way lying through fields thickly set with great towns, two or three of them to be seen from one. He sent word by an Indian to the Cacique, that he was coming to obtain his friendship and to consider him as a brother; to which he received for answer, that he would be welcomed; that he would be received with special good-will, and all that his lordship required of him should be done; and the Chief sent him on the road a present of skins, shawls, and fish. After these gifts were made, all the towns into which the Governor came were found occupied; and the inhabitants awaited him in peace, offering him skins, shawls, and fish.

Accompanied by many persons, the Cacique

came half a league on the road from the town where he dwelt to receive the Governor, and, drawing nigh to him, thus spoke:

VERY HIGH, POWERFUL, AND RENOWNED MASTER:

I greet your coming. So soon as I had notice of you, your power and perfections, although you entered my territory capturing and killing the dwellers upon it, who are my vassals, I determined to conform my wishes to your will, and hold as right all that you might do, believing that it should be so for a good reason, providing against some future event, to you perceptible but from me concealed; since an evil may well be permitted to avoid another greater, that good can arise, which I trust will be so; for from so excellent a prince, no bad motive is to be suspected. My ability is so small to serve you, according to your great merit, that though you should consider even my abundant will and humility in proffering you all manner of services, I must still deserve little in your sight. If this ability can with reason be valued, I pray you receive it, and with it my country and my vassals, of me and them disposing at your pleasure; for though you were lord of the earth, with no more good-will would you be received, served, and obeyed.

The Governor responded appropriately in a few words which satisfied the Chief. Directly they fell to making each other great proffers, using much courtesy, the Cacique inviting the Governor to go and take lodging in his houses. He excused himself, the better to preserve peace, saying that he wished to lie in the field; and, because the heat was excessive, he pitched the camp among some trees, quarter of a league from the town. The Cacique went to his town, and returned with many Indians singing, who, when they had come to where the Governor was, all prostrated themselves. Among them were two blind men. The Cacique made an address, of which, as it was long, I will give the substance in a few words. He said, that inasmuch as the Governor was son of the Sun, he begged him to restore sight to those Indians: whereupon the blind men arose, and they very earnestly entreated him to do so. Soto answered them, that in the heavens above there was One who had the power to make them whole, and do whatever they could ask of Him, whose servant he was; that this great Lord made the sky and the earth, and man after His image; that He had suffered on the tree of the true cross to save the human race, and risen from the grave on the third day,—what of man there was of Him dying, what of divinity being immortal; and that, having ascended into heaven, He was there with open arms to receive all that would be converted to Him. He then directed a lofty cross of wood to be made and set up in the highest part of the town, declaring to the Cacique that the Christians worshipped that, in the form and memory of the one on which Christ suffered. He placed himself with his people before it, on their knees, which the Indians did likewise; and he told them that from that time thenceforth they should thus worship the Lord, of whom he had spoken to them, that was in the skies, asking Him for whatsoever they stood in need.

The Chief being asked what was the distance to Pacaha, he answered that it was one day's journey, and said that on the extreme of his territory there was a lake, like an estuary, that entered into the Rio Grande, to which he would send persons in advance to build a bridge, whereby they might pass over it. The night of the day the Governor left, he slept at a town of Casqui; and the next day he passed in sight of two other towns, and arrived at the lake, which was half a cross-bow-shot over, of great depth and swiftness of current. The Indians had just got done the bridge as he came up. It was built of wood, in the manner of timber thrown across from tree to tree; on one side there being a rail of poles, higher than the rest, as a support for those who should pass. The Cacique of Casqui having come with his people, the Governor sent word by an Indian to the Cacique of Pacaha, that though he might be at enmity with him of Casqui, and that Chief be present, he should receive neither injury nor insult, provided that he attended in peace and desired his friendship, for as a brother would he treat him. The Indian went as he was bid, and returned, stating that the Cacique took no notice of the message, but that he fled out of the town, from the back part, with all his people. Then the Governor entered there, and with the cavalry charged in the direction the Indians were running, and at another town, a quarter of a league off, many were taken. As fast as they were captured, the horsemen delivered them to the Indians of Casqui, who, from being their enemies, brought them with great heed and pleasure to the town where the Christians were, greatly regretting that they had not the liberty to kill them. Many shawls, deer-skins, lion and bear-skins, and many cat-skins were found in the town. Numbers who had been a long time badly covered, there clothed themselves. Of the shawls they made mantles and cassocks; some made gowns and lined them with cat-skins, as they also did the cassocks. Of the deer-skins were made jerkins, shirts, stockings, and shoes; and from the bear-skins they made very good cloaks, such as no water could get through. They found shields of raw cow-hide out of which armour was made for the horses.

CHAPTER XXIIII

OF HOW THE CACIQUE OF PACAHA CAME IN PEACE,
AND HE OF CASQUI, HAVING ABSENTED HIMSELF,
RETURNED TO EXCUSE HIS CONDUCT; AND HOW
THE GOVERNOR MADE FRIENDSHIP BETWEEN THE
CHIEFS.

ON Wednesday, the nineteenth day[1] of
June, the Governor entered Pacaha, and took
quarters in the town where the Cacique was
accustomed to reside. It was enclosed and
very large. In the towers and the palisade
were many loopholes. There was much dry
maize, and the new was in great quantity,
throughout the fields. At the distance of half
a league to a league off were large towns, all
of them surrounded with stockades.

Where the Governor stayed was a great
lake, near to the enclosure; and the water
entered a ditch that well-nigh went round the
town. From the River Grande to the lake
was a canal, through which the fish came into
it, and where the Chief kept them for his
eating and pastime. With nets that were
found in the place, as many were taken as

[1] The nineteenth of June, in 1541, was Sunday.
It should be Wednesday, the twenty-ninth. *Cf.*
Ranjel, Vol. II. p. 139. Probably in the original publication of the text XIX. was printed instead of XXIX. (B.)

need required; and however much might be the casting, there was never any lack of them. In the many other lakes about were also many fish, though the flesh was soft, and none of it so good as that which came from the river. The greater number differ from those in the fresh water of Spain. There was a fish called bagre, the third part of which was head, with gills from end to end, and along the sides were great spines, like very sharp awls. Those of this sort that lived in the lake were as big as pike; in the river were some that weighed from one hundred to one hundred and fifty pounds. Many were taken with the hook. There was one in the shape of barbel; another like bream, with the head of a hake, having a colour between red and brown, and was the most esteemed. There was likewise a kind called peel-fish, the snout a cubit in length, the upper lip being shaped like a shovel. Another fish was like a shad. Except the bagres and the peel, they were all of scale. There was one, called pereo, the Indians sometimes brought, the size of a hog, and had rows of teeth above and below.

The Cacique of Casqui many times sent large presents of fish, shawls, and skins. Having told the Governor that he would deliver into his hands the Cacique of Pacaha, he went to Casqui, and ordered many canoes to ascend

the river, while he should march by land, taking many of his warriors. The Governor,
with forty cavalry and sixty infantry, was
conducted by him up stream; and the Indians
who were in the canoes discovered the Cacique of Pacaha on an islet between two arms
of the river. Five Christians entered a canoe,
of whom was Don Antonio Osorio, to go in
advance and see what number of people the
Cacique had with him. There were five or
six thousand souls, who, directly as they saw
the people, taking the Indians who went in
the canoes to be Christians also, the Cacique,
and as many as could get into three canoes
that were there, fled to the opposite bank;
the greater part of the rest, in terror and confusion, plunging into the river to swim, many,
mostly women and infants, got drowned.
Then the Governor, who was on land, without
knowing what was passing with Don Antonio and those who accompanied him, ordered
the Christians, in all haste, to enter the canoes
with the Indians of Casqui, and they directly
joining Don Antonio on the islet, many men
and women were taken, and much clothing.

Many clothes, which the Indians had in
cane hurdles and on rafts to carry over,
floated down stream, the people of Casqui
filling their canoes with them; and, in fear
that the Christians might take these away,

their Chief went off with them down the river to his territory, without taking leave. At this the Governor became indignant, and directly returning to Pacaha, two leagues on the road, he overran the country of Casqui, capturing twenty or thirty of its men. The horses being tired, and there remaining no time that day to go farther, he went on to Pacaha, with the intention of marching in three or four days upon Casqui, directly letting loose a man of Pacaha, sending word by him to its Chief, that should he desire his friendship to come to him, and together they would go to carry war upon Casqui: and immediately there arrived many people of Pacaha, bringing as the chief an Indian, who was exposed by a prisoner, brother of the Cacique. The Governor told them that their lord must come; that he well knew that Indian was not he; for that nothing could be done without its being known to him before they so much as thought of it. The Cacique came the next day, followed by many Indians, with a large gift of fish, skins, and shawls. He made a speech, that all were glad to hear, and concluded by saying, that although his lordship had causelessly inflicted injury on his country and his subjects, he did not any the less cease to be his, and was always at his command. The Governor ordered his brother to

be let go, and some principal men he held
captives. That day a messenger arrived from
Casqui, saying that his master would come
early on the morrow to excuse the error he
had committed in going away without his
license; to which the Governor bade him say,
in return, to the Cacique, that if he did not
come himself in person he would go after
him, and inflict the punishment he deserved.

The Chief of Casqui came the next day,
and after presenting many shawls, skins, and
fish, he gave the Governor a daughter, saying
that his greatest desire was to unite his blood
with that of so great a lord as he was, begging that he would take her to wife. He
made a long and discreet oration, full of praise
of Soto; and concluded by asking his forgive-
ness, for the love of that cross he had left,
for having gone off without his permission;
that he had done so because of the shame
he felt for what his people had done without
his consent. The Governor said that he had
taken a good sponsor; that he had himself
determined, if the Cacique had not come to
apologize, to go after him and burn his towns,
kill him and his people, and lay waste his
country. To this the Chief replied:

MASTER:

I and mine belong to you; and my territory is
yours, so that you will destroy it, if you will, as

your own, and your people you will slay. All that
falls from your hand I shall receive as from my
lord's, and as merited chastisement. Know, that the
service you have done me in leaving that cross has
been signal, and more than I have deserved; for,
you know, of great droughts the maize in our fields
was perishing, and no sooner had I and mine thrown
ourselves on our knees before it, asking for water,
than the want was supplied.

The Governor made friendship between the
Chiefs of Casqui and Pacaha, and placed them
at the table, that they should eat with him.
They had a difficulty as to who should sit at
his right hand, which the Governor quieted by
telling them that among the Christians the one
seat was as good as the other; that they
should so consider it, and while with him no
one should understand otherwise, each taking
the seat he first came to. Thence he sent
thirty horsemen and fifty footmen to the
Province of Caluça, to see if in that direction
they could turn back towards Chisca, where
the Indians said there was a foundry of gold
and copper. They travelled seven days
through desert, and returned in great extremity, eating green *ameixas* and maize-stalks,
which they had found in a poor town of seven
or eight houses. The Indians stated that
thence towards the north, the country, being
very cold, was very thinly populated; that
cattle were in such plenty, no maize-field

could be protected from them, and the inhabitants lived upon the meat. Seeing that the country was so poor off for maize that there could be no support, the Governor asked the Indians in what direction there were most inhabitants; and they said that they had knowledge of a large province and a country of great abundance, called Quiguate, that lay in the southern direction.

CHAPTER XXV

How the Governor went from Pacaha to Aquiguate and to Coligoa, and came to Cayas.

THE Governor rested in Pacaha forty days, during which time the two Caciques made him presents of fish, shawls, and skins, in great quantity, each striving to outdo the other in the magnitude of the gifts. At the time of his departure, the Chief of Pacaha bestowed on him two of his sisters, telling him that they were tokens of love, for his remembrance, to be his wives. The name of one was Macanoche, that of the other Mochila. They were symmetrical, tall, and full: Macanoche bore a pleasant expression; in her manners and features appeared the lady; the other was robust. The Cacique of Casqui ordered the bridge to be repaired; and the Governor, returning through his territory, lodged in the field near his town. He brought there much fish, exchanged two women for as many shirts with two of the Christians, and furnished a guide and tamemes. The Governor marched to one of his towns, and slept, and the next night came to another that was near a river, where he ordered him to bring canoes, that he might cross over. There taking his leave, the Chief went back.

The Governor travelled towards Aquiguate, and on the fourth day of August came to the residence of the Cacique, who, although he had sent him a present, on the road, of many shawls and skins, abandoned the place through fear on his arrival. That town was the largest seen in Florida: one-half of it was occupied by the Governor and his people; and, after a few days, discovering that the Indians were dealing in falsehoods, he ordered the other part to be burned, that it might not afford them cover should they attack him at night, nor be an embarrassment to his cavalry in a movement to repel them. An Indian having come, attended by a multitude, declaring himself to be the Cacique, the Governor delivered him over to be looked after by his body-guard. Many of the Indians went off, and returned with shawls and skins; but, finding small opportunity for carrying out their evil plan, one day the pretended Cacique,

walking out of the house with the Governor,
ran away with such swiftness that not one of
the Christians could overtake him; and plunging into the river, at the distance of a crossbow-shot from the town, he made for the
other shore, where many Indians, giving loud
shouts, began to make use of their arrows.
The Governor directly crossed over to attack
them with horse and foot; but they dared
not await him: following them up, he came
to a town that was abandoned, before which
there was a lake the horses could not pass over,
and on the other side were many females.
The footmen having crossed, capturing many
of them, took much clothing. Returning to
the camp early in the night, the sentinels
seized a spy, who assenting to the request to
lead to where the Cacique was, the Governor
directly set out with twenty cavalry and fifty
infantry in quest of him. After travelling a
day and a half, they found him in a thick
wood; and a soldier, ignorant of who he
was, having struck him on the head with a
cutlass, he called out not to kill him, that he
was the Chief; so he was captured, and with
him one hundred and forty of his people.

The Governor, returning to Quiguate,
directed him to tell his people to come and
serve the Christians; but, after waiting some
days, in the hope of their arrival, and finding

that they did not come, he sent two captains, each on an opposite side of the river, with infantry and cavalry, whereby many of both sexes were made prisoners. The Indians, seeing the harm that they received for their rebellious conduct, waited on the Governor to take his commands, coming and going often, bringing with them presents of fish. The Cacique and two of his wives being at their liberty in the quarters of the Governor, which were guarded by his halberdiers, he asked them what part of the country was most inhabited; to which they replied, that to the south, or down the river, where were large towns, and the Caciques governed wide territories, with numerous people; and that to the northwest was a province, near some mountains, called Coligoa. He, with the others, deemed it well to go thither first; saying that the mountains, perhaps, would make a difference in the soil, and that silver and gold might afterward follow.

The country of Aquiguate, like that of Casqui and Pacaha, was level and fertile, having rich river margins, on which the Indians made extensive fields. From Tascaluça to the River Grande may be three hundred leagues; a region very low, having many lakes: from Pacha to Quiguate there may be one hundred and ten leagues. There he left

the Cacique in his own town; and an Indian
guided them through an immense pathless
thicket of desert for seven days, where they
slept continually in ponds and shallow pud-
dles. Fish were so plentiful in them that they
were killed with blows of cudgels; and as the
Indians travelled in chains, they disturbed the
mud at the bottom, by which the fish, becoming stupefied, would swim to the surface, when
as many were taken as were desired.

The inhabitants of Coligoa had never heard
of the Christians, and when these got so near
their town as to be seen, they fled up stream
along a river that passed near by there; some
throwing themselves into the water, whence
they were taken by their pursuers, who, on
either bank, captured many of both sexes, and
the Cacique with the rest. Three days from
that time came many Indians, by his order,
with offerings of shawls, deer-skins, and two
cowhides: they stated that at the distance of
five or six leagues towards the north were
many cattle, where the country, being cold,
was thinly inhabited; and that, to the best of
their knowledge, the province that was better
provisioned than any other, and more populous, was one to the south, called Cayas.

About forty leagues from Quiguate stood
Coligoa, at the foot of a mountain, in the vale
of a river of medium size, like the Caya, a

stream that passes through Estremadura. The soil was rich, yielding maize in such profusion that the old was thrown out of store to make room for the new grain. Beans and pumpkins were likewise in great plenty: both were larger and better than those of Spain: the pumpkins, when roasted, have nearly the taste of chestnuts. The Cacique continued behind in his own town, having given a guide for the way to Cayas.

We travelled five days, and came to the Province of Palisema. The house of the Cacique was canopied with coloured deerskins, having designs drawn on them, and the ground was likewise covered in the same manner, as if with carpets. He had left it in that state for the use of the Governor, a token of peace, and of a desire for friendship, though still he did not dare to await his coming. The Governor, finding that he had gone away, sent a captain with horse and foot to look after him; and though many persons were seen, because of the roughness of the country, only a few men and boys were secured. The houses were few and scattered: only a little maize was found.

Directly the Governor set forward and came to Tatalicoya, whence he took the Cacique, who guided him to Cayas, a distance of four days' journey from that town. When he arrived and saw the scattered houses, he thought, from the information he had received of the great populousness of the country, that the Cacique was lying to him—that it was not the province; and he menaced him, bidding him tell where he was. The Chief, as likewise the other Indians taken near by, declared that to be in Cayas, the best town in all the province; and that although the houses were far apart, the country occupied being extensive, it had numerous people and many maize-fields. The town was called Tanico. The camp was placed in the best part of it, nigh a river. On the day of arrival, the Governor, with some mounted men, went a league farther, but found no one, and only some skins, which the Cacique had put on the road to be taken, a sign of peace, by the usage of the country.

CHAPTER XXVI

How the Governor went to visit the Province of Tulla, and what happened to him.

THE Governor tarried a month in the Province of Cayas. In this time the horses fattened and throve more than they had done at other places in a longer time, in consequence of the large quantity of maize there. The blade of it, I think, is the best fodder that grows. The beasts drank so copiously from the very warm and brackish lake, that they came having their bellies swollen with the leaf when they were brought back from watering. To that spot the Christians had wanted salt: they now made a quantity and took it with them. The Indians carry it into other parts, to exchange for skins and shawls.

The salt is made along by a river, which, when the water goes down, leaves it upon the sand. As they cannot gather the salt without a large mixture of sand, it is thrown together into certain baskets they have for the purpose, made large at the mouth and small at the bottom. These are set in the air on a ridge-pole; and water being thrown on, vessels are placed under them wherein it may fall; then, being strained and placed on the fire, it is boiled away, leaving salt at the bottom.

The lands on the shores of the river were fields, and maize was in plenty. The Indians dared not cross the river to where we were. Some appearing, were called to by the soldiers who saw them, and having come over were conducted by them before the Governor. On being asked for the Cacique, they said that he was peaceful but afraid to show himself. The Governor directly sent them back to tell him to come, and, if he desired his friendship,

to bring an interpreter and a guide for the
travel before them; that if he did not do so
he would go in pursuit, when it would be the
worse for him. The Governor waited three
days, and finding that the Cacique did not
come, he went in pursuit and brought him
there a captive, with one hundred and fifty
of his people. He asked him if he had knowledge of any great cacique, and in what direction the country was most inhabited. The
Indian stated, that the largest population
about there was that of a province lying to
the southward, thence a day and a half's
travel, called Tulla; that he could give him
a guide, but no interpreter; that the tongue
of that country was different from his,
and that he and his ancestors had ever
been at war with its chiefs, so that they neither conversed together nor understood each
other.

Then the Governor, with cavalry and fifty
infantry, directly set out for Tulla, to see if
it were such a land as he might pass through
with his troops. So soon as it became known
that he had reached there, the inhabitants
were summoned; and as they gathered by
fifteen and twenty at a time, they would come
to attack the Christians. Finding that they
were sharply handled, and that in running
the horses would overtake them, they got upon

the house-tops, where they endeavoured to
defend themselves with their bows and arrows.
When beaten off from one roof, they would
get up on to another; and the Christians while
going after some, others would attack them
from an opposite direction. The struggle
lasted so long that the steeds, becoming tired,
could not be made to run. One horse was
killed and others were wounded. Of the
Indians fifteen were slain, and forty women
and boys made prisoners; for to no one who
could draw a bow and could be reached was
his life spared him.

The Governor determined at once to go
back, before the inhabitants should have time
to come together. That afternoon he set out,
and travelling into the night, he slept on the
road to avoid Tulla, and arrived the next day
at Cayas. Three days later he marched to
Tulla, bringing with him the Cacique, among
whose Indians he was unable to find one who
spoke the language of that place. He was
three days on the way, and at his arrival
found the town abandoned, the inhabitants
not venturing to remain for him. But no
sooner did they know that he was in the town,
than, at four o'clock on the morning of the
first night, they came upon him in two
squadrons, from different directions, with
bows and arrows and with long staves like

pikes. So soon as they were felt, both cavalry and infantry turned out. Some Christians and some horses were injured. Many of the Indians were killed.

Of those made captive, the Governor sent six to the Cacique, their right hands and their noses cut off, with the message, that, if he did not come to him to apologize and render obedience, he would go in pursuit, and to him, and as many of his as he might find, would he do as he had done to those he sent. He allowed him three days in which to appear, making himself understood by signs, in the best manner possible, for want of an interpreter. At the end of that time an Indian, bearing a back-load of cow-skins from the Cacique, arrived, weeping with great sobs, and coming to where the Governor was, threw himself at his feet. Soto raised him up, and the man made a speech, but there was none to understand him. The Governor, by signs, told him to return and say to the Cacique, that he must send him some one who could speak with the people of Cayas. Three Indians came the next day with loads of cow-skins, and three days afterward came twenty others. Among them was one who understood those of Cayas. After a long oration from him, of apologies for the Cacique and in praise of the Governor, he concluded by say-

ing, that he with the others had come, in behalf of the Chief, to inquire what his lordship
would command, for that he was ready to
serve him.

At hearing these words the Governor and
the rest were all rejoiced; for in no way
could they go on without a guide. He ordered the man to be safely kept, and told the
Indians who came with him to go back to the
Cacique and say, that he forgave him the past
and greatly thanked him for the interpreter
and the presents; that he should be pleased to
see him, and to come the next day, that they
might talk together. He came at the end of
three days, and with him eighty Indians. As
he and his men entered the camp they wept,—
the token of obedience and the repentance of
of a past error, according to the usage of that
country. He brought a present of many cow-
skins, which were found very useful; the
country being cold, they were taken for bed-
covers, as they were very soft and the wool
like that of sheep. Near by, to the northward, are many cattle. The Christians did
not see them, nor go where they were, because it was a country thinly populated, having little maize. The Cacique of Tulla made
an address to the Governor, in which he
apologized and offered him his country, his
vassals, and his person. The speech of this

Cacique—like those of the other chiefs, and all the messengers in their behalf who came before the Governor—no orator could more elegantly phrase.

CHAPTER XXVII

How the Governor went from Tulla to Autiamque, where he passed the Winter.

THE Governor informed himself of the country in every direction. He ascertained that toward the west there was a thin population, and to the southeast were great towns, principally in a province, abundant of maize, called Autiamque, at the distance of about eighty leagues, ten days' journey from Tulla. The winter was already come. The cold, rain, and snow did not permit the people to travel for two or three months in the year, and the Governor feared to remain among that sparse population, lest his force could not be subsisted for that length of time. Moreover, the Indians said that near Autiamque was a great water, which, from their account, appeared to him to be an arm of the sea. Hence, he determined to winter in that province, and in the following summer to go to the sea-side, where he would build two brigantines,—one to send to Cuba, the other to New Spain, that the arrival of either might bear tidings of him. Three years had elapsed since he had been heard of by Doña Ysabel, or by any person in a civilized community. Two hundred and fifty men of his were dead, likewise one hundred and fifty horses. He desired to recruit from Cuba of man and beast, calculating, out of his property there, to refit and again go back to advance, to discover and to conquer farther on towards the west, where he had not reached, and whither Cabeça de Vaca had wandered.

Having dismissed the Caciques of Tulla and Cayas, the Governor took up his course, marching five days over very sharp mountains, and arrived in a peopled district called Quipana. Not a native could be captured, because of the roughness of the country, and the town was among ridges. At night an ambuscade was set, in which two men were taken, who said that Autiamque was six days' journey distant, and that there was another province toward the south, eight days' travel off, called Guahate, very abundant in maize and very populous. However, as Autiamque was nearer, and most of the Indians spoke of it, the Governor continued on his journey thither.

At the end of three days he came to a town called Anoixi. Having sent a captain in advance, with thirty horse and fifty foot, they came suddenly upon the inhabitants, taking many of both sexes. On the second day afterwards, the Governor arrived at another town, called Catamaya, and slept in the adjacent fields. Two Indians coming to him from the Cacique, with the pretext of a message, in order to ascertain his business, he told them to say to their master, that he wished to speak with him; but they came no more, nor was other word returned. The next day the Christians went to the town, which was without people, and having taken what maize they needed, that night they reached a wood to rest, and the day following arrived at Autiamque.

They found in store much maize, also beans, walnuts, and dried *ameixas* in large quantities. Some Indians were taken while gathering up their clothing, having already carried away their wives. The country was level and very populous. The Governor lodged in the best portion of the town, and ordered a fence immediately to be put up about the encampment, away from the houses, that the Indians without might do no injury with fire. Measuring off the ground by pacing, he allotted to each his part to build, according to the Indians he possessed; and the timber being soon brought by them, in three days it was finished, made of very high trees sunk deep in the ground, and traversed by many pieces.

Near by passed a river of Cayas, the shores of it well peopled, both above and below the town. Indians appeared on the part of the Cacique with a present of shawls and skins, and a lame Chief, the lord of a town called Tietiquaquo, subject to the Cacique of Autiamque, came frequently to visit the Governor, and brought him gifts of the things he possessed. The Cacique sent to the Governor to inquire what length of time he would remain in his territory; and hearing that he was to be there more than three days, he sent no more messages nor Indians, but treated with the lame Chief to insurge. Numerous inroads were made, in which many persons of both sexes were taken, and among the rest that Chief, whom the Governor, having reprehended and admonished, set at liberty, in consideration of the presents he had made, giving him two Indians to bear him away on their shoulders.

The Cacique of Autiamque, desiring to drive the strangers out of his territory, ordered spies to be set about them. An Indian, coming at night to the entrance of the palisade, was noticed by a soldier on guard, who, putting himself behind the door as he entered, struck him down with a cutlass. When taken before the Governor, he was asked why he came, but fell dead without utterance. The next night the Governor sent a soldier to beat the alarm, and cry out that he saw Indians, in order to ascertain how fast the men would hasten to the call. This was done also in other places, at times when it appeared to him they were careless, that he might reprove those who were late in coming; so that for danger, as well as for doing his duty, each one on such occasion would strive to be the first.

The Christians stayed three months in Autiamque, enjoying the greatest plenty of maize, beans, walnuts, and dried *ameixas;* also conies, which they had never had ingenuity enough to ensnare until the Indians there taught them. The contrivance is a strong spring, that lifts the animal off its feet, a noose being made of a stiff cord to run about the neck, passing through rings of cane, that it may not be gnawed. Many of them were taken in the maize-fields, usually when it was freezing or snowing. The Christians were there a month in snow, when they did not go out of town, save to a wood, at the distance of two crossbow-shots, to which, whenever fuel was wanted, a road was opened, the Governor and others, on horseback, going to and returning from it many times, when it was brought from there by those on foot. In this time many conies were killed with arrows by the Indians, who were now allowed to go at large in their shackles. The animal is of two sorts; one of them like that of Spain, the other of the colour, form, and size of the great hare, though longer even, and having bigger loins.

CHAPTER XXVIII

How the Governor went from Autiamque to Nilco, and thence to Cuachoya.

On Monday, the sixth day of March, of the year 1542 of the Christian era, the Governor set out from Autiamque to seek Nilco, which the Indians said was nigh the River Grande, with the purpose, by going to the sea, to recruit his forces. He had not over three hundred efficient men, nor more than forty horses. Some of the beasts were lame, and useful only in making out the show of a troop of cavalry; and, from the lack of iron, they had all gone a year without shoes, though, from the circumstance of travelling in a smooth country, they had little need of them.

Juan Ortiz died in Autiamque, a loss the Governor greatly regretted; for, without an interpreter, not knowing whither he was travelling, Soto feared to enter the country, lest he might get lost. Thenceforth a lad, taken in Cutifachiqui, who had learned somewhat of the language of the Christians, served as the interpreter. The death was so great a hindrance to our going, whether on discovery or out of the country, that to learn of the Indians what would have been rendered in four words, it became necessary now to have the whole day: and oftener than otherwise the very opposite was understood of what was asked; so that many times it happened the road that we travelled one day, or sometimes two or three days, would have to be returned over, wandering up and down, lost in thickets.

The Governor went to a province called Ayays, arriving at a town near the river that passed by Cayas, and by Autiamque, from which he had been ten days in coming. He ordered a piragua to be built, in which he crossed; and, having arrived on the other shore, there set in such weather that marching was impossible for four days, because of snow. When that ceased to fall, he travelled three days through desert, a region so low, so full of lakes and bad passages, that at one time, for the whole day, the travel lay through water up to the knees at places, in others to the stirrups; and occasionally, for the distance of a few paces, there was swimming. And he came to Tutelpinco, a town untenanted, and found to be without maize, seated near a lake that flowed copiously into the river with a violent current. Five Christians, in charge of a captain, in attempting to cross, by order of the Governor, were upset; when some seized hold of the canoe they had employed, others of trees that grew in the water, while one, a worthy man, Francisco Bastian, a native of Villanueva de Barcarota, became drowned. The Governor travelled all one day along the margin of the lake, seeking for a ford, but could discover none, nor any way to get over.

Returning to Tutelpinco at night, the Governor found two friendly natives, who were willing to show him the crossing, and the road he was to take. From the reeds and timber of the houses, rafts and causeways were made, on which the river was crossed. After three days' marching, at Tianto, in the territory of Nilco, thirty Indians were taken, among whom were two Chiefs of the town. A captain, with infantry and cavalry, was directly dispatched to Nilco, that the inhabitants might not have time to carry off their provisions. In going through three or four large towns, at the one where the Cacique resided, two leagues from where the Governor stayed, many Indians were found to be in readiness, with bows and arrows, who, surrounding the place, appeared to invite an onset; but so soon as they saw the Christians drawing nigh to them without faltering, they approached

the dwelling of the Cacique, setting fire to
it, and, by a pond near the town, through
which the horses could not go, they fled.

The following day, Wednesday, the
twenty-ninth of March, the Governor arrived
at Nilco, making his quarters, and those of
his people, in the town of the Cacique, which
was in an open field, that for a quarter of a
league over was all inhabited; and at the distance of from half a league to a league off
were many other large towns, in which was a
good quantity of maize, beans, walnuts, and
dried *ameixas*. This was the most populous
of any country that was seen in Florida, and
the most abundant in maize, excepting Coça
and Apalache. An Indian, attended by a
party, arrived at the camp, and, presenting
the Governor with a cloak of marten-skins
and a string of pearls, he received some mar-
garidetas (a kind of bead much esteemed in
Peru), and other trinkets, with which he was
well pleased. At leaving, he promised to be
back in two days, but did not return. In the
night-time, however, the Indians came in
canoes, and carrying away all the maize they
could take, set up their huts on the other side
of the river, among the thickest bushes. The
Governor, finding that the Indians did not
arrive within the time promised, ordered an
ambuscade to be placed at some cribs, near

the lake, to which the Indians came for maize.
Two of them were taken, who told him that
the person who had come to visit him was
not the Cacique, but one sent by him, pre-
tending to be he, in order to observe what
might be the vigilance of the Christians, and
whether it was their purpose to remain in that
country, or to go farther. Directly a captain,
with men on horseback and foot, were sent
over to the other shore; but, as their crossing was observed, only ten or a dozen Indians,
of both sexes, could be taken; and with these
the Christians returned to camp.

This river, passing by Anilco, is the same
that flows by Cayas and Autiamque, and falls
into the River Grande, which flows by Pacaha
and Aquixo, near the Province of Guachoya,
the lord of which ascended in canoes to carry
war upon him of Nilco. In his behalf a messenger came to the Governor, saying that the
Cacique was his servant, desiring to be so
considered, and that in two days from that
time he would come to make his salutation.
He arrived in season, accompanied by some
of his principal men, and with great proffers
and courtesy, he presented many shawls and
deer-skins. The Governor gave him some
articles of barter, showing him much attention, and inquired what towns there might
be on the river below. He replied that he

knew of none other than his own; that opposite was the Province of a Cacique called
Quigaltam; then, taking his leave, returned
to his town.

The Governor determined to go to Guachoya within a few days, to learn if the sea
were near, or if there were any inhabited
territory nigh it, where he might find subsistence whilst those brigantines were building, that he desired to send to a country of
Christians. As he crossed the River of Nilco,
there came up Indians in canoes from
Guachoya, who, when they saw him, thinking that he was in their pursuit, to do them
harm, they returned down the river, and
informed the Cacique, when he took away
from the town whatsoever his people could
carry, and passed over with them, all that
night, to the other bank of the River Grande.
The Governor sent a captain with fifty men,
in six canoes, down the river to Guachoya;
while he, with the rest, marched by land,
arriving there on Sunday, the seventeenth day [1]
of April. He took up his quarters in the town
of the Cacique, which was palisaded, seated
a crossbow-shot from the stream, that is there
called the River Tamaliseu, Tapatu at Nilco,
Mico at Coça, and at its entrance is known
as The River.

[1] Sunday was the fifteenth of April. (B.)

CHAPTER XXIX

THE MESSAGE SENT TO QUIGALTAM, AND THE AN-
SWER BROUGHT BACK TO THE GOVERNOR, AND
WHAT OCCURRED THE WHILE.

So soon as the Governor arrived in
Guachoya, he ordered Juan de Añasco, with
as many people as could go in the canoes, to
ascend the river; for while they were coming
from Anilco they saw some cabins newly built
on the opposite shore. The Comptroller went,
and brought back the boats laded with maize,
beans, dried *ameixas,* and the pulp of them
made into many loaves. The same day an
Indian arrived from Guachoya, and said that
the Cacique would come on the morrow. The
next day, many canoes were seen ascending
the river; and the people in them remained
for an hour on the opposite side of the River
Grande, in consultation, as to whether they
should come to us or not; but finally they
concluded to come, and crossed the river,
among them being the Cacique of Guachoya
with many Indians, bringing much fish, many
dogs, skins, and blankets. So soon as they had
landed, they went to the lodging of the Governor in the town, and having presented him
with the offerings, the Cacique thus spoke:

POTENT AND EXCELLENT MASTER:

I entreat you to forgive me the error I committed

in going away from this town, and not waiting to greet and to obey you; since the occasion should have been for me, and is, one of pride: but I dreaded what I should not have feared, and did consequently what was out of reason; for error comes of haste, and I left without proper thought. So soon as I had reflected, I resolved not to follow the inclination of the foolish, which is to persist in his course, but to take that of the discreet and the wise: thus have I changed my purpose, coming to see in what it is you will bid me serve you, within the farthermost limits of my control.

The Governor received him with much pleasure, thanking him for the proffers and gift. Being asked if he had any information of the sea, he said, none, nor of any other inhabited country below on that side of the river, except a town two leagues distant, belonging to a chief subject to him; nor on the other shore, save three leagues down, the Province of Quigaltam, the lord of which was the greatest of that country. The Governor, suspecting that the Cacique spoke untruthfully, to rid his towns of him, sent Juan de Añasco with eight of cavalry down the river, to discover what population might be there, and get what knowledge there was of the sea. He was gone eight days, and stated, when he got back, that in all that time he could not travel more than fourteen or fifteen leagues, on account of the great

bogs that came out of the river, the cane-
brakes and thick scrubs there were along the
margin, and that he had found no inhabited
spot.

The Governor sank into a deep despondency
at sight of the difficulties that presented themselves to his reaching the sea; and, what was
worse, from the way in which the men and
horses were diminishing in numbers, he could
not sustain himself in the country without
succour. Of that reflection he pined: but,
before he took to his pallet, he sent a messenger to the Cacique of Quigaltam, to say that
he was the child of the Sun, and whence he
came all obeyed him, rendering their tribute;
that he besought him to value his friendship,
and to come where he was; that he would
be rejoiced to see him; and in token of love
and his obedience, he must bring him something from his country that was in most
esteem there. By the same Indian, the Chief
returned this answer:

As to what you say of your being the son of the
Sun, if you will cause him to dry up the great river,
I will believe you: as to the rest, it is not my custom to visit any one, but rather all, of whom I
have ever heard, have come to visit me, to serve and
obey me, and pay me tribute, either voluntarily or
by force: if you desire to see me, come where I am;
if for peace, I will receive you with special good-
will; if for war, I will await you in my town; but

neither for you, nor for any man, will I set back one foot.

When the messenger returned, the Governor was already low, being very ill of fevers. He grieved that he was not in a state to cross the river at once, and go in quest of the Cacique, to see if he could not abate that pride; though the stream was already flowing very powerfully, was nearly half a league broad, sixteen fathoms in height, rushing by in furious torrent, and on either shore were many Indians; nor was his power any longer so great that he might disregard advantages, relying on his strength alone.

Every day the Indians of Guachoya brought fish, until they came to be in such plenty that the town was covered with them.

The Governor having been told by the Cacique, that on a certain night, the Chief of Quigaltam would come to give him battle, he suspected it to be a fiction of his devising to get him out of his country, and he ordered him to be put under guard, and from that night forth the watch to be well kept. When asked why the Chief did not come, he said that he had, but that, finding the Governor in readiness, he dared not adventure; and he greatly importuned him to send the captains over the river, offering to supply many men to go upon Quigaltam; to which the Governor

said, that so soon as he got well he would himself go to seek that Cacique. Observing how
many Indians came every day to the town, and
how populous was that country, the Governor
fearing that they would plot together, and
practise on him some perfidy, he permitted the
gates in use, and some gaps in the palisade that
had not yet been closed up, to remain open,
that the Indians might not suppose he stood
in fear, ordering the cavalry to be distributed
there; and the night long they made the
round, from each squadron going mounted
men in couples to visit the scouts, outside
the town, at points in the roads, and to the
crossbow-men that guarded the canoes in
the river.

That the Indians might stand in terror of
them, the Governor determined to send a captain to Nilco, which the people of Guachoya
had told him was inhabited, and, treating the
inhabitants there severely, neither town would
dare to attack him: so he commanded Captain Nuño de Tobar to march thither with
fifteen horsemen, and Captain Juan de Guzman, with his company of foot, to ascend the
river by water in canoes. The Cacique of Guachoya ordered canoes to be brought, and many
warriors to come, who went with the Christians. Two leagues from Nilco, the cavalry,
having first arrived, waited for the foot, and

thence together they crossed the river in the night. At dawn, in sight of the town, they came upon a scout, who, directly as he saw the Christians, set up loud yells, and fled to carry the news to those in the place. Nuño de Tobar, and those with him, hastened on so rapidly, that they were upon the inhabitants before they could all get out of town. The ground was open field; the part of it covered by the houses, which might be a quarter of a league in extent, contained five or six thousand souls. Coming out of them, the Indians ran from one to another habitation, numbers collecting in all parts, so that there was not a man on horseback who did not find himself amidst many; and when the Captain ordered that the life of no male should be spared, the surprise was such, that there was not a man among them in readiness to draw a bow. The cries of the women and children were such as to deafen those who pursued them. About one hundred men were slain; many were allowed to get away badly wounded, that they might strike terror into those who were absent.

Some persons were so cruel and butcher-like that they killed all before them, young and old, not one having resisted little nor much; while those who felt it their duty to be wherever there might be resistance, and were esteemed brave, broke through the crowds of Indians, bearing down many with their stirrups and the breasts of their horses, giving some a thrust and letting them go, but encountering a child or a woman would take and deliver it over to the footmen. To the ferocious and bloodthirsty, God permitted that their sin should rise up against them in the presence of all—when there was occasion for fighting showing extreme cowardice, and in the end paying for it with their lives.

Eighty women and children were captured at Nilco, and much clothing. The Indians of Guachoya, before arriving at the town, had come to a stop, and from without watched the success of the Christians over the inhabitants; and when they saw that these were scattered, that the cavalry were following and lancing them, they went to the houses for plunder, filling the canoes with clothing; and lest the Christians might take away what they got, they returned to Guachoya, where they came greatly astonished at what they had seen done to the people of Nilco, which they, in great fear, recounted circumstantially to their Cacique.

CHAPTER XXX

THE DEATH OF THE ADELANTADO, DON HERNANDO DE SOTO, AND HOW LUYS MOSCOSO DE ALVARADO WAS CHOSEN GOVERNOR.

THE Governor, conscious that the hour approached in which he should depart this life, commanded that all the King's officers should be called before him, the captains and the principal personages, to whom he made a speech. He said that he was about to go into the presence of God, to give account of all his past life; and since He had been pleased to take him away at such a time, and when he could recognize the moment of his death, he, His most unworthy servant, rendered Him hearty thanks. He confessed his deep obligations to them all, whether present or absent, for their great qualities, their love and loyalty to his person, well tried in the sufferance of hardship, which he ever wished to honour, and had designed to reward, when the Almighty should be pleased to give him repose from labour with greater prosperity to his fortune. He begged that they would pray for him, that through mercy he might be pardoned his sins, and his soul be received in glory: he asked that they would relieve him of the charge he held over them, as well of the indebtedness he was under to them all, as to forgive him any wrongs they might have received at his hands. To prevent any divisions that might arise, as to who should command, he asked that they would be pleased to elect a principal and able person to be governor, one with whom they should all be satisfied, and, being chosen, they would swear before him to obey: that this would greatly satisfy him, abate somewhat the pains he suffered, and moderate the anxiety of leaving them in a country, they knew not where.

Baltasar de Gallegos responded in behalf of all, consoling him with remarks on the shortness of the life of this world, attended as it was by so many toils and afflictions, saying that whom God earliest called away, He showed particular favour; with many other things appropriate to such an occasion: And finally, since it pleased the Almighty to take him to Himself, amid the deep sorrow they not unreasonably felt, it was necessary and becoming in him, as in them, to conform to the Divine Will: that as respected the election of a governor, which he ordered, whomsoever his Excellency should name to the command, him would they obey. Thereupon the Governor nominated Luys Moscoso de Alvarado to be his Captain-General; when by all those present was he straightway chosen and sworn Governor.

The next day, the twenty-first of May, departed this life the magnanimous, the virtuous, the intrepid Captain, Don Hernando de Soto, Governor of Cuba and Adelantado of Florida. He was advanced by fortune, in the way she is wont to lead others, that he might fall the greater depth: he died in a land, and at a time, that could afford him little comfort in his illness, when the danger of being no more heard from stared his companions in the face, each one himself having need of sympathy, which was the cause why they neither gave him their companionship nor visited him, as otherwise they would have done.

Luys de Moscoso determined to conceal what had happened from the Indians; for Soto had given them to understand that the Christians were immortal; besides, they held him to be vigilant, sagacious, brave; and, although they were at peace, should they know him to be dead, they, being of their nature inconstant, might venture on making an attack; and they were credulous of all that he had told them, who made them believe that some things which went on among them privately, and he had come at without their being able to see how, or by what means, that the figure which appeared in a mirror he showed, told him whatsoever they might be about, or desired to do; whence neither by

word nor deed did they dare undertake any
thing to his injury.

So soon as the death had taken place, Luys
de Moscoso directed the body to be put
secretly into a house, where it remained three
days; and thence it was taken at night, by
his order, to a gate of the town, and buried
within. The Indians, who had seen him ill,
finding him no longer, suspected the reason;
and passing by where he lay, they observed the
ground loose, and, looking about, talked
among themselves. This coming to the
knowledge of Luys de Moscoso, he ordered
the corpse to be taken up at night, and among
the shawls that enshrouded it having cast
abundance of sand, it was taken out in a
canoe and committed to the middle of the
stream. The Cacique of Guachoya asked
for him, saying: "What has been done with
my brother and lord, the Governor?" Luys
de Moscoso told him that he had ascended into
the skies, as he had done on other many occasions; but as he would have to be detained
there some time, he had left him in his stead.
The Chief, thinking within himself that he
was dead, ordered two well-proportioned
young men to be brought, saying, that it was
the usage of the country, when any lord died,
to kill some persons, who should accompany
and serve him on the way, on which account

they were brought; and he told him to command their heads to be struck off, that they might go accordingly to attend his friend and master. Luys de Moscoso replied to him, that the Governor was not dead, but only gone into the heavens, having taken with him of his soldiers sufficient number for his need, and he besought him to let those Indians go, and from that time forward not to follow so evil a practice. They were presently ordered to be let loose, that they might return to their houses; but one of them refused to leave, alleging that he did not wish to remain in the power of one who, without cause, condemned him to die, and that he who had saved his life he desired to serve so long as he should live.

Luys de Moscoso ordered the property of the Governor to be sold at public outcry. It consisted of two male and three female slaves, three horses, and seven hundred swine. For each slave, or horse, was given two or three thousand cruzados, to be paid at the first melting up of gold or silver, or division of vassals and territory, with the obligation that should there being nothing found in the country, the payment should be made at the end of a year, those having no property to pledge to give their bond. A hog brought in the same way trusted, two hundred cruzados. Those who had left any thing at home bought more sparingly, and took less than others. From that time forward most of the people owned and raised hogs; they lived on pork, observed Fridays and Saturdays, and the vespers of holidays, which they had not done before; for, at times, they had passed two or three months without tasting any meat, and on the day they got any, it had been their custom to eat it.

CHAPTER XXXI

How the Governor Luys de Moscoso left Guachoya and went to Chaguate, and from thence to Aguacay.

Some were glad of the death of Don Hernando de Soto, holding it certain that Luys de Moscoso, who was given to leading a gay life, preferred to see himself at ease in a land of Christians, rather than continue the toils of war, discovering and subduing, which the people had come to hate, finding the little recompense that followed. The Governor ordered that the captains and principal personages should come together, to consult and determine upon what they would do; and, informed of the population there was on all sides, he found that towards the west the country was most inhabited, and that descending the stream, after passing Quigaltam, it was desert and had little subsistence. He besought them all to give him their opinion in writing, signed with their names, that, having the views of every one, he might determine whether to follow down the river or enter the land.

To every one it appeared well to march westwardly, because in that direction was New Spain, the voyage by sea being held more hazardous and of doubtful accomplishment, as a vessel of sufficient strength to weather a storm could not be built, nor was there captain nor pilot, needle nor chart, nor was it known how distant might be the sea; neither had they any tidings of it, or if the river did not take some great turn through the land, or might not have some fall over rocks where they might be lost. Some, who had seen the sea-card, found that by the shore, from the place where they were to New Spain, there should be about five hundred leagues; and they said that by land, though they might have to go round-about sometimes, in looking for a peopled country, unless some great impassable wilderness should intervene, they could not be hindered from going forward that summer; and, finding provision for support in some peopled country where they might stop, the following summer they should arrive in a land of Christians; and that, going by land, it might be they should discover some rich country which would avail them. Moscoso, although it was his desire to get out of the land of Florida in the shortest time, seeing the difficulties that lay before him in a voyage by sea, determined to undertake that which should appear to be the best to all.

Monday, the fifth of June, the Governor left Guachoya, receiving a guide from the Cacique who remained in his town. They passed through a province called Catalte; and, going through a desert six days' journey in extent, on the twentieth of the month they came to Chaguate. The Cacique of the province had been to visit the Governor, Don Hernando de Soto, at Autiamque, where he took him presents of shawls, skins, and salt. The day before Luys de Moscoso arrived, a sick Christian becoming missed, whom the Indians were suspected to have killed, he sent word to the Cacique to look for and return him—that in so doing he would continue to be his friend; if otherwise, the Cacique should not hide from him anywhere, nor he nor his, and that he would leave his country in ashes. The Chief directly came, and, bringing the Christian, with a large gift of shawls and skins, he made this speech:

EXCELLENT MASTER:

I would not deserve that opinion you have of me for all the wealth of the world. Who impelled me to visit and serve that excellent lord, the Governor, your father, in Autiamque, which you should have remembered, where I offered myself, with all loyalty, truth, and love, to serve and obey his life-time: or what could have been my purpose, having received favours of him, and without either of you having done me any injury, that I should be moved to do that which I should not? Believe me, no outrage, nor worldly interest, could have been equal to making me act thus, or could have so blinded me. Since, however, in this life, the natural course is, after one pleasure should succeed many pains, fortune has been pleased with your indignation to moderate the joy I felt in my heart at your coming, and have failed where I aimed to hit, in pleasing this Christian, who remained behind lost, treating him in a manner of which he shall himself speak, thinking that in this I should do you service, and intending to come with and deliver him to you at Chaguate, serving you in all things, to the extent possible in my power. If for this I deserve punishment from your hand, I shall receive it, as coming from my master's, as though it were favour.

The Governor answered, that because he had not found him in Chaguate he was incensed, supposing that he had kept away, as others had done; but that, as he now knew his loyalty and love, he would ever consider him a brother, and would favour him in all matters. The Cacique went with him to the town where he resided, the distance of a day's journey. They passed through a small town where was a lake, and the Indians made salt:

the Christians made some on the day they rested there, from water that rose near by from springs in pools. The Governor was six days in Chaguate, where he informed himself of the people there were to the west. He heard that three days' journey distant, was a province called Aguacay.

On leaving Chaguate, a Christian remained behind, named Francisco de Guzman, bastard son of a gentleman of Sevilla, who, in fear of being made to pay for gaming debts in the person of an Indian girl, his concubine, he took her away with him; and the Governor, having marched two days before he was missed, sent word to the Cacique to seek for and send him to Aguacay, whither he was marching, but the Chief never did. Before arriving at this province, they received five Indians, coming with a gift of skins, fish, and roasted venison, sent on the part of the Cacique. The Governor reached his town on Wednesday, the fourth day of July,[1] and finding it unoccupied, lodged there. He remained in it a while, making some inroads, in which many Indians of both sexes were captured. There they heard of the South Sea. Much salt was got out of the sand, gathered in a vein of earth-like slate, and was made as they make it in Cayas.

[1] Wednesday was the fifth of July. (B.)

CHAPTER XXXII

How the Governor went from Aguacay to
Naguatex, and what happened to him.

THE day the Governor left Aguacay he
went to sleep near a small town, subject to
the lord of that province. He set the encampment very nigh a salt lake, and that
afternoon some salt was made. He marched
the next day, and slept between two mountains,
in an open grove; the next after, he arrived
at a small town called Pato; and on the fourth
day of his departure from Aguacay he came
to the first inhabited place, in a province called
Amaye. There they took an Indian, who
said that thence to Naguatex was a day and a
half's journey, all the way lying through an
inhabited region.

Having passed out of Amaye, on Saturday,
the twentieth of July,[1] between that place and
Naguatex, at mid-day, along a clump of luxuriant woods, the camp was seated. From
thence Indians being seen, who had come to
espy them, those on horseback went in their
pursuit, killed six, and captured two. The
prisoners being asked by the Governor why
they had come, they said, to discover the
numbers he had, and their condition, having

[1] Saturday was the twenty-second of July. (B.)

been sent by their lord, the Chief of Nagua-tex; and that he, with other caciques, who came in his company and his cause, had determined on giving him battle that day.

While thus conferring, many Indians advanced, formed in two squadrons, who, so soon as they saw that they were descried, giving whoops, they assailed the Christians with great fury, each on a different quarter; but finding how firm was the resistance, they turned, and fleeing, many lost their lives; the greater part of the cavalry pursuing them, forgetful of the camp, when those that remained were attacked by other two squadrons, that had lain in concealment, who, in their turn, having been withstood, paid the penalty that the first had done.

When the Christians came together, after the Indians fled, they heard loud shouting, at the distance of a crossbow-shot from where they were; and the Governor sent twelve cavalry to see what might be the cause. Six Christians were found amidst numerous Indians, two, that were mounted, defending four on foot, with great difficulty; and they, as well as those who went to their succour, finally ended by killing many. They had got lost from those who followed after the first squadrons, and, in returning to the camp, fell among them with whom they were found fighting. One Indian, brought back alive, being asked by the Governor who they were that had come to give him battle, said the Cacique of Naguatex, the one of Maye, and another of a province called Hacanac, lord of great territories and numerous vassals, he of Naguatex being in command. The Governor, having ordered his right arm to be cut off, and his nose, sent him to the Cacique, with word that he would march the next day into his territory to destroy it, and that if he wished to dispute his entrance to await him.

The Governor stopped there that night, and the following day he came to the habitations of Naguatex, which were much scattered, and having asked for the town of the Cacique, he was told that it stood on the opposite side of a river near by. He marched thitherward; and coming to the river, on the other bank he saw many Indians awaiting him, set in order to defend the passage; but, as he did not know whether it might be forded or not, nor whereabouts it could be crossed, and having some wounded men and horses, he determined to repose for some time in the town where he was, until they should be healed.

In consequence of the great heats that prevailed, he pitched his camp a quarter of a league from the river, in a fine open grove of high trees, near a brook, close to the town.

Some Indians taken there, having been asked if the river was fordable, said yes, at times it was, in certain places; on the tenth day he sent two captains, each with fifteen cavalry, one up and the other down the stream, with guides to show where they might get over, to see what towns were to be found on the opposite side. They were both opposed by the Indians, who defended the passages the best they could; but these being taken notwithstanding, on the other shore they found many habitations, with much subsistence; and having seen this, the detachments went back to the camp.

CHAPTER XXXIII

How the Cacique of Naguatex came to visit the Governor, and how the Governor went thence, and arrived at Nondacao.

From Naguatex, where the Governor was, he sent a message to the Cacique, that, should he come to serve and obey him, he would pardon the past; and if he did not, he would go to look after him, and would inflict the chastisement he deserved for what he had done. At the end of two days the Indian got back, bringing word that to-morrow the Cacique would come. The day before his arrival, the Chief sent many Indians in advance of him,

among whom were some principal men, to discover in what mood the Governor was, and
determine whether he would himself come or
not. They went back directly as they had an-
nounced his approach, the Cacique arriving in
a couple of hours afterward, well attended by
his people. They came one before another,
in double file, leaving an opening through the
midst, where he walked. They arrived in the
Governor's presence weeping, after the usage
of Tula (thence to the eastward not very distant), when the Chief, making his proper
obeisance, thus spoke:

VERY HIGH AND POWERFUL LORD, WHOM ALL THE
    EARTH SHOULD SERVE AND OBEY:
    I venture to appear before you, after having been
guilty of so great and bad an act, that, for only
having thought of it, I merit punishment. Trusting in your greatness, although I do not deserve
pardon, yet for your own dignity you will show
me mercy, having regard to my inferiority in comparison with you, forgetting my weakness, which
to my sorrow, and for my greater good, I have
come to know.
    I believe that you and yours must be immortal;
that you are master of the things of nature; since
you subject them all, and they obey you, even the
very hearts of men. Witnessing the slaughter and
destruction of my men in battle, which came of my
ignorance, and the counsel of a brother of mine,
who fell in the action, from my heart did I re-
pent the error that I committed, and directly I

desired to serve and obey you: wherefore have I come, that you may chastise and command me as your own.

The Governor replied, that the past would be forgiven; and that, should he thenceforward do his duty, he would be his friend, favouring him in all matters.

At the end of four days Luys de Moscoso set forward, and arrived at a river he could not pass, it ran so full, which to him appeared wonderful at the time, more than a month having gone by since there had been rain. The Indians said, that it often increased in that manner, without there being rain anywhere, in all the country. It was supposed to be caused by the sea entering in; but he learned that the water always flowed from above, and that the Indians nowhere had any information of the sea.

The Governor returned back to where he had been the last days; and, at the end of eight more, understanding that the river might then be crossed, he left, and passed over to the other bank, where he found houses, but no people. He lodged out in the fields, and sent word to the Cacique to come where he was, and to give him a guide to go on with. After some days, finding that the Cacique did not come, nor send any one, he dispatched two captains, each of them in a different direction, to set fire to the towns, and seize the people that might be found. They burned much provision, and captured many Indians. The Cacique, seeing the damage his territories were receiving, sent five principal men to Moscoso, with three guides, who understood the language farther on, whither he would go.

Directly the Governor set out from Naguatex, arriving, on the third day, at a hamlet of four or five houses, belonging to the Cacique of the poor province named Nissohone, a thinly peopled country, having little maize. Two days' journey on the way, the Indians who guided the Governor, in place of taking him to the west, would lead him to the east, and at times they went through heavy thickets, out of the road: in consequence, he ordered that they should be hanged upon a tree. A woman, taken in Nissohone, served as the guide, who went back to find the road.

In two days' time the Governor came to another miserable country, called Lacane. An Indian was taken, who said the land of Nondacao was very populous, the houses much scattered, as in mountainous regions, and there was plenty of maize. The Cacique came with his Indians, weeping, as those of Naguatex had done, which is, according to their custom, significant of obedience; and he made a present of much fish, offering to do whatsoever

might be required of him. He took his departure, leaving a guide for the Province of
Soacatino.

CHAPTER XXXIIII

How the Governor marched from Nondacao to
Soacatino and Guasco, passing through a
Wilderness, whence, for want of a Guide
and Interpreter, he retired to Nilco.

The Governor set out from Nondacao for
Soacatino, and on the fifth day came to a province called Aays. The inhabitants had never
heard of the Christians. So soon as they observed them entering the territory the people
were called out, who, as fast as they could get
together, came by fifties and hundreds on the
road, to give battle. While some encountered
us, others fell upon our rear; and when we
followed up those, these pursued us. The
attack continued during the greater part of
the day, until we arrived at their town. Some
men were injured, and some horses, but nothing so as to hinder travel, there being not
one dangerous wound among all. The Indians suffered great slaughter.

The day on which the Governor departed,
the guide told him he had heard it said in
Nondacao, that the Indians of Soacatino had
seen other Christians; at which we were all

delighted, thinking it might be true, and that they could have come by the way of New Spain; for if it were so, finding nothing in Florida of value, we should be able to go out of it, there being fear we might perish in some wilderness. The Governor, having been led for two days out of the way, ordered that the Indian be put to the torture, when he confessed that his master, the Cacique of Nondacao, had ordered him to take them in that manner, we being his enemies, and he, as his vassal, was bound to obey him. He was commanded to be cast to the dogs, and another Indian guided us to Soacatino, where we came the following day.

The country was very poor, and the want of maize was greatly felt. The natives being asked if they had any knowledge of other Christians, said they had heard that near there, towards the south, such men were moving about. For twenty days the march was through a very thinly peopled country, where great privation and toil were endured; the little maize there was, the Indians having buried in the scrub, where the Christians, at the close of the day's march, when they were well weary, went trailing, to seek for what they had need of it to eat.

Arrived at a province called Guasco, they found maize, with which they loaded the horses and the Indians; thence they went to another settlement, called Naquiscoça, the inhabitants of which said that they had no knowledge of any other Christians. The Governor ordered them put to torture, when they stated that farther on, in the territories of another chief, called Naçacahoz, the Christians had arrived, and gone back toward the west, whence they came. He reached there in two days, and took some women, among whom was one who said that she had seen Christians, and, having been in their hands, had made her escape from them. The Governor sent a captain with fifteen cavalry to where she said they were seen, to discover if there were any marks of horses, or signs of any Christians having been there; and after travelling three or four leagues, she who was the guide declared that all she had said was false; and so it was deemed of everything else the Indians had told of having seen Christians in Florida.

As the region thereabout was scarce of maize, and no information could be got of any inhabited country to the west, the Governor went back to Guasco. The residents stated, that ten days' journey from there, toward the sunset, was a river called Daycao, whither they sometimes went to drive and kill deer, and whence they had seen persons on

the other bank, but without knowing what
people they were. The Christians took as
much maize as they could find, to carry with
them; and journeying ten days through a
wilderness, they arrived at the river of which
the Indians had spoken. Ten horsemen sent
in advance by the Governor had crossed; and,
following a road leading up from the bank,
they came upon an encampment of Indians
living in very small huts, who, directly as they
saw the Christians, took to flight, leaving
what they had, indications only of poverty
and misery. So wretched was the country,
that what was found everywhere, put together,
was not half an alqueire of maize. Taking
two natives, they went back to the river, where
the Governor waited; and on coming to ques-
tion the captives, to ascertain what towns there
might be to the west, no Indian was found in
the camp who knew their language.

The Governor commanded the captains and
principal personages to be called together that
he might determine now by their opinions what
was best to do. The majority declared it
their judgment to return to the River Grande
of Guachoya, because in Anilco and thereabout was much maize; that during the
winter they would build brigantines, and the
following spring go down the river in them
in quest of the sea, where having arrived, they

would follow the coast thence along to New Spain,—an enterprise which, although it appeared to be one difficult to accomplish, yet from their experience it offered the only course to be pursued. They could not travel by land, for want of an interpreter; and they considered the country farther on, beyond the River Daycao, on which they were, to be that which Cabeça de Vaca had said in his narrative should have to be traversed, where the Indians wandered like Arabs, having no settled place of residence, living on prickly pears, the roots of plants, and game; and that if this should be so, and they, entering upon that tract, found no provision for sustenance during winter, they must inevitably perish, it being already the beginning of October; and if they remained any longer where they were, what with rains and snow, they should neither be able to fall back, nor, in a land so poor as that, to subsist.

The Governor, who longed to be again where he could get his full measure of sleep, rather than govern and go conquering a country so beset for him with hardships, directly returned, getting back from whence he came.

CHAPTER XXXV

How the Christians returned to Nilco, and
thence went to Minoya, where they prepared to build Vessels in which to leave
Florida.

When what had been determined on was
proclaimed in the camp, many were greatly
disheartened. They considered the voyage by
sea to be very hazardous, because of their poor
subsistence, and as perilous as was the journey
by land, whereon they had looked to find a
rich country, before coming to the soil of the
Christians. This was according to what
Cabeça de Vaca told the Emperor, that after
seeing cotton cloth, would be found gold,
silver, and stones of much value, and they were
not yet come to where he had wandered; for
before arriving there, he had always travelled
along the coast, and they were marching far
within the land; hence by keeping toward the
west they must unavoidably come to where
he had been, as he said that he had gone about
in a certain region a long time, and marched
northward into the interior. Now, in Guasco,
they had already found some turkoises, and
shawls of cotton, which the Indians gave them
to understand, by signs, were brought from
the direction of the sunset; so that they who

should take that course must approach the country of Christians.

There was likewise much other discontent. Many grieved to go back, and would rather have continued to run the peril of their lives than leave Florida poor. They were not equal, however, to changing what was resolved on, as the persons of importance agreed with the Governor. There was one, nevertheless, who said afterwards that he would willingly pluck out an eye, to put out another for Luys de Moscoso, so greatly would he grieve to see him prosper; with such bitterness did he inveigh against him and some of his friends, which he would not have dared to do, only he knew that in a couple of days from that time the government would have to be relinquished.

From Daycao, where they were, to the Rio Grande, was a distance of one hundred and fifty leagues, towards which they had marched always westwardly; and, as they returned over the way, with great difficulty could they find maize to eat; for, wheresoever they had passed, the country lay devastated, and the little that was left, the Indians had now hidden. The towns they had burned in Naguatex, of which they had repented, they found already rebuilt, and the houses full of maize. That country is populous and abun-

dant. Pottery is made there of clay, little differing from that of Estremoz or Montemor.

To Chaguate, by command of the Cacique,
the Indians came in peace, and said, that the
Christian who had remained there would not
come. The Governor wrote to him, sending
ink and paper, that he might answer. The
purport of the letter stated his determination
to leave Florida, reminded him of his being a
Christian, and that he was unwilling to leave
him among heathen; that he would pardon the
error he had committed in going to the Indians, should he return; and that if they
should wish to detain him, to let the Governor
know by writing. The Indian who took the
letter came back, bringing no other response
than the name and rubric of the person written
on the back, to signify that he was alive. The
Governor sent twelve mounted men after him;
but, having his watchers, he so hid himself
that he could not be found. For want of
maize the Governor could not tarry longer
to look for him; so he left Chaguete, crossed
the river at Aays, and following it down, he
discovered a town which they had not seen
before, called Chilano.

They came to Nilco, where the Governor
found so little maize, that there was not
enough to last while they made the vessels;
for during seed-time, while the Christians

were in Guachoya, the Indians, in fear of them, had not dared to come and plant the grounds; and no other land about there was known to have maize, that being the most fertile region of the vicinity, and where they had the most hope of finding sustenance. Everybody was confounded.

Many thought it bad counsel to have come back from the Daycao, and not to have taken the risk of continuing in the way they were going by land; as it seemed impossible they should escape by sea, unless a miracle might be wrought for them; for there was neither pilot nor sea-chart; they knew not where the river entered the sea, nor of the sea could they get any information; they had nothing out of which to make sails, nor for rope a sufficiency of enequen (a grass growing there, which is like hemp), and what they did find was saved for calk; nor was there wherewith to pitch them. Neither could they build vessels of such strength that any accident might not put them in jeopardy of life; and they greatly feared what befell Narvaez, who was lost on the coast, might happen to them also. But the most of all they feared was the want of maize; for without that they could not support themselves, or do anything they would. All were in great dismay.

The Christians chose to commend them-

selves to God for relief, and beseech Him to
point them out a way by which they might
be saved. By His Goodness He was pleased
that the people of Anilco should come peacefully, and state that two days' journey thence,
near the River Grande, were two towns of
which the Christians had not heard, in a
fertile country named Aminoya; but whether
it then contained maize or not, they were
unable to tell, as they were at war with those
places; they would nevertheless be greatly
pleased to go and destroy them, with the aid
of the Christians. The Governor sent a captain thither, with horsemen and footmen, and
the Indians of Anilco. Arriving at Aminoya,
he found two large towns in a level, open
field, half a league apart, in sight of each
other, where he captured many persons, and
found a large quantity of maize. He took
lodging in one of the towns, and directly sent
a message to the Governor concerning what
he had found, with which all were well content. They set out from Anilco in the beginning of December, and on that march, as
well as before coming there from Chilano,
they underwent great exposure; for they passed
through much water, and rain fell many times,
bringing a north wind, with severe cold, so
that when in the field they had the water both
above and below them; and if at the end of a

day's journey they found dry ground to lie upon, they had occasion to be thankful. In these hardships nearly all the Indians in service died, and also many Christians, after coming to Aminoya; the greater number being sick of severe and dangerous diseases, marked with inclination to lethargy. André de Vasconcelos died there, and two Portugues brothers of Elvas, near of kin to him, by the name of Soti.

The Christians chose for their quarters what appeared to be the best town: it was stockaded, and stood a quarter of a league distant from the Rio Grande. The maize that lay in the other town was brought there, and when together the quantity was estimated to be six thousand fanegas. For the building of ships better timber was found than had been seen elsewhere in all Florida; on which account, all rendered many thanks to God for so signal mercy, encouraging the hope in them, that they should be successful in their wish to reach a shore of Christians.

CHAPTER XXXVI

How Seven Brigantines were built, and the Christians took their Departure from Aminoya.

So soon as the Christians arrived in Aminoya, the Governor commanded the chains to

be collected which every one brought along
for Indians, the iron in shot, and what was
in the camp. He ordered a furnace to be set
up for making spikes, and likewise timber to
be cut down for the brigantines. A Portugues, of Ceuta, had learned to saw lumber
while a captive in Fez; and saws had been
brought for that purpose, with which he taught
others, who assisted him. A Genoese, whom
God had been pleased to spare (as without
him we could not have gone away, there being
not another person who knew how to con-
struct vessels), built the brigantines with the
help of four or five Biscayan carpenters, who
hewed the plank and ribs for him; and two
calkers, one a Genoese, the other a Sardinian,
closed them up with the oakum, got from a
plant like hemp, called enequen, of which I
have before spoken; but from its scarcity the
flax of the country was likewise used, as well
as the ravellings of shawls. The cooper
sickened to the point of death, and there was
not another workman; but God was pleased
to give him health, and notwithstanding he
was very thin, and unfit to labour, fifteen days
before the vessels sailed, he had made for each
of them two of the half-hogsheads sailors call
quartos, four of them holding a pipe of
water.

The Indians of a province called Tagoanate,

two days' journey up the river, likewise those of Anilco and Guachoya, and other neighbouring people, seeing the vessels were building, thought, as their places of concealment were by the water's side, that it was the purpose to come in quest of them; and because the Governor had asked for shawls, as necessary out of which to make sails, they came often, and brought many, as likewise a great deal of fish.

Of a verity, it did appear that God chose to favour the Christians in their extreme need, disposing the Indians to bring the garments; otherwise, there had been no way but to go and fetch them. Then the town where they were, as soon as the winter should set in, would become so surrounded by water, and isolated, that no one could travel from it by land farther than a league, or a league and a half, when the horses could no longer be used. Without them we were unable to contend, the Indians being so numerous; besides, man to man on foot, whether in the water or on dry ground, they were superior, being more skilful and active, and the conditions of the country more favourable to the practice of their warfare.

They also brought us ropes; and the cables needed were made from the bark of the mulberry-trees. Anchors were made of stirrups, for which others of wood were substituted.

In March, more than a month having passed since rain fell, the river became so enlarged that it reached Nilco, nine leagues off; and the Indians said, that on the opposite side it also extended an equal distance over the country.

The ground whereon the town stood was higher, and where the going was best, the water reached to the stirrups. Rafts were made of trees, upon which were placed many boughs, whereon the horses stood; and in the houses were like arrangements; yet, even this not proving sufficient, the people ascended into the lofts; and when they went out of the houses it was in canoes, or, if on horseback, they went in places where the earth was highest.

Such was our situation for two months, in which time the river did not fall, and no work could be done. The natives, coming in canoes, did not cease to visit the brigantines. The Governor, fearing they would attack him in that time, ordered one of those coming to the town to be secretly seized, and kept until the rest were gone; which being done, he directed that the prisoner should be tortured, in order to draw out from him any plotting of treason that might exist. The captive said, that the Caciques of Nilco, Guachoya, Taguanate, and others, in all some twenty, had determined to come upon him, with a great body of people. Three days before they should do so, the better to veil their evil purpose and perfidy, they were to send a present of fish; and on the day itself, another present was to be sent in advance of them, by some Indians, who, with others in the conspiracy, that were serving, should set fire to the houses, after getting possession of the lances placed near the doors of the dwellings, when the Caciques, with all their people, being concealed in the thicket nigh the town, on seeing the flame, should hasten to make an end of them.

The Governor ordered the Indian to be put in a chain; and on the day that was stated, thirty men having come with fish, he commanded their right hands to be cut off, sending word by them to the Cacique of Guachoya, whose they were, that he and his might come when they pleased, he desired nothing better, but they should learn that they could not think of a thing that he did not know their thought before them. At this they were all greatly terrified; the Caciques of Nilco and Taguanate came to make excuses, and a few days after came the Cacique of Guachoya, with a principal Indian, his vassal, stating that he had certain information of an agreement between the Caciques of Nilco and Taguanate to come and give the Christians battle.

So soon as some Indians arrived from Nilco, the Governor questioned them, and they confirming what was said, he delivered them at once to the principal Indian of Guachoya, who took them out of the town and killed them. The next day came others from Taguanate, who likewise having confessed, the Governor commanded that their right hands and their noses should be cut off, and he sent them to the Cacique. With this procedure the people of Guachoya were well satisfied, and often came with presents of shawls and fish, and of hogs, which were the breeding of some sows lost there the year before. Having persuaded the Governor to send people to Taguanate, so soon as the waters fell, they brought canoes, in which infantry went down the river, and a captain proceeded by land with cavalry; and having guided them until they came to Taguanate, the Christians assaulted the town, took many men and women, and shawls, which, with what they had already, sufficed for their want.

In the month of June the brigantines were finished, and the Indians having stated that the river rose but once in the year, which was with the melting of snow, that had already passed, it being now summer, and a long time since rain had fallen, God was pleased that the water should come up to the town, where the

vessels were, whence they floated into the river;
for had they been taken over ground, there
would have been danger of tearing open the
bottoms, thereby entirely wrecking them, the
planks being thin, and the spikes made short
for the lack of iron.

In the time that the Christians were there,
the people of Aminoya came to offer their service, being compelled by hunger to beg some
ears of that corn which had been taken from
them. As the country was fertile, they were
accustomed to subsist on maize; and as all
that they possessed had been seized, and the
population was numerous, they could not
exist. Those who came to the town were
weak, and so lean that they had not flesh on
their bones, and many died near by, of clear
hunger and debility. The Governor ordered,
under pain of heavy punishments, that maize
should not be given to them; still, when it was
seen that they were willing to work, and that
the hogs had a plenty, the men, pitying their
misery and destitution, would share their grain
with them; so that when the time arrived for
departure, there was not enough left to answer
for what was needed. That which remained
was put into the brigantines and the great
canoes, which were tied together in couples.
Twenty-two horses were taken on board, being
the best there were in the camp; the flesh of

the rest was jerked, as was also that of the hogs that remained. On the second day of July, of the year one thousand five hundred and forty-three, we took our departure from Aminoya.

CHAPTER XXXVII

How the Christians, on their Voyage, were at-tacked in the River, by the Indians of Quigualtam, and what happened.

THE day before the Christians left Ami-noya, it was determined to dismiss the men and women that were serving, with the exception of some hundred slaves, more or less, put on board by the Governor, and by those he favoured. As there were many persons of condition, whom he could not refuse what he allowed to others, he made use of an artifice, saying, that while they should be going down the river they might have the use of them; but on coming to the sea they would have to be left, because of the necessity for water, and there were but few casks; while he secretly told his friends to take the slaves, that they would carry them to New Spain. All those to whom he bore ill-will, the greater number, not suspecting his concealment from them, which after a while appeared, thought it in-human for so short service, in return for so

NARRATIVES OF DE SOTO

much as the natives had done, to take them
away, to be left captives out of their territories,
in the hands of other Indians, abandoning five
hundred males and females, among whom were
many boys and girls who understood and
spoke Spanish. The most of them wept,
which caused great compassion, as they were
all Christians of their own free will, and were
now to remain lost.

In seven brigantines went three hundred
and twenty-two Spaniards from Aminoya.
The vessels were of good build, except that
the planks were thin, on account of the shortness of the spikes; and they were not pitched,
nor had they decks to shed the water that
might enter them, but planks were placed
instead, upon which the mariners might run
to fasten the sails, and the people accommodate
themselves above and below.

The Governor appointed his captains, giving to each of them his brigantine, taking
their word and oath to obey him until they
should come to the land of Christians. He
chose for himself the brigantine he liked best.
On the day of his departure they passed by
Guachoya, where the Indians, in canoes, were
waiting for them in the river, having made
a great arbour on the shore, to which they
invited him, but he made excuse, and passed
along. They accompanied him until arriving

where an arm of the river extends to the right, near which they said was Quigualtam; and they importuned him to go and make war upon it, offering their assistance. As they told him there were three days' journey down the river to that province, suspecting they had arranged some perfidy, he dismissed them there; then, submitting himself to where lay the full strength of the stream, went his voyage, driven on rapidly by the power of the current and aid of oars.

On the first day they came to land in a clump of trees, by the left bank, and at dark they retired to the vessels. The following day they came to a town, where they went on shore, but the occupants dared not tarry for them. A woman who was captured, being questioned, said the town was that of a chief named Huhasene, a subject of Quigualtam, who, with a great many people, was waiting for them. Mounted men went down the river, and finding some houses, in which was much maize, immediately the rest followed. They tarried there a day, in which they shelled and got ready as much maize as was needed. In this time many Indians came up the river in canoes; and, on the opposite side, in front, somewhat carelessly put themselves in order of battle. The Governor sent after them the crossbow-men he had with him, in two canoes, and as many other persons as they could hold, when the Indians fled; but, seeing the Spaniards were unable to overtake them, returning, they took courage, and, coming nearer, menaced them with loud yells. So soon as the Christians retired, they were followed by some in canoes, and others on land, along the river; and, getting before them, arrived at a town near the river's bluff, where they united, as if to make a stand. Into each canoe, for every brigantine was towing one at the stern for its service, directly entered some men, who, causing the Indians to take flight, burned the town. Soon after, on the same day, they went on shore in a large open field, where the Indians dared not await their arrival.

The next day a hundred canoes came together, having from sixty to seventy persons in them, those of the principal men having awnings, and themselves wearing white and coloured plumes, for distinction. They came within two crossbow-shot of the brigantines, and sent a message in a small canoe, by three Indians, to the intent of learning the character of the vessels, and the weapons that we use. Arriving at the brigantine of the Governor, one of the messengers got in, and said that he had been sent by the Cacique of Quigaltam, their lord, to commend him, and to make

known that whatever the Indians of Guachoya
had spoken of him was falsely said, they being
his enemies; that the Chief was his servant,
and wished to be so considered. The Governor told him that he believed all that he
had stated to be true; to say so to him,
and that he greatly esteemed him for his
friendship.

With this the messengers went to where
the others, in the canoes, were waiting for
them; and thence they all came down yelling,
and approached the Spaniards with threats.
The Governor sent Juan de Guzman, captain
of foot, in the canoes, with twenty-five men
in armour, to drive them out of the way. So
soon as they were seen coming, the Indians,
formed in two parts, remained quietly until
they were come up with, when, closing, they
took Juan de Guzman, and those who came
ahead with him, in their midst, and, with
great fury, closed hand to hand with them.
Their canoes were larger than his, and many
leaped into the water—some to support them,
others to lay hold of the canoes of the Spaniards, to cause them to capsize which was
presently accomplished, the Christians falling
into the water, and, by the weight of their
armour, going to the bottom; or when one by
swimming, or clinging to a canoe, could sustain himself, they with paddles and clubs,

striking him on the head, would send him below.

When those in the brigantines who witnessed the defeat desired to render succour, the force of the stream would not allow them to return. One brigantine, which was that nighest to the canoes, saved four men, who were all of those that went after the Indians who escaped. Eleven lost their lives; among whom was Juan de Guzman and a son of Don Carlos, named Juan de Vargas. The greater number of the others were also men of consideration and of courage. Those who escaped by swimming said, that they saw the Indians get into the stern of one of their canoes with Juan de Guzman, but whether he was carried away dead or alive, no one could state.

CHAPTER XXXVIII

How the Christians were pursued by the Indians.

The natives, finding they had gained a victory, took so great encouragement that they proceeded to attack the brigantines, which they had not dared to before. They first came up with one in the rear-guard, commanded by Calderon, and at the first volley of arrows twenty-five men were wounded. There were only four on board in armour, who went

to the side of the vessel for its defence. Those
unprotected, finding how they were getting
hurt, left the oars, placing themselves below
under the cover; and the brigantine, beginning
to swing about, was going where the current
of water chanced to take her, when one of the
men in armour, seeing this, without waiting
the captain's order, made one of the infantry
take the oar and steer, while he stood before
to cover him with his shield. The Indians
afterwards came no nearer than bow-shot,
whence they could assail without being assaulted, or receiving injury, there being in
each brigantine only a single crossbow much
out of order; so that the Christians had little
else to do than to stand as objects to be shot
at, watching for the shafts. The natives,
having left this brigantine, went to another,
against which they fought for half an hour:
and one after another, in this way they ran
through with them all.

The Christians had mats with them to lie
upon of two thicknesses, very close and strong,
so that no arrow could pierce them, that, when
safety required, were hung up; and the Indians, finding that these could not be traversed,
directed their shafts upward, that, exhausted,
fell on board, inflicting some wounds. Not
satisfied with this, they strove to get at the
men with the horses; but the brigantines were

brought about the canoes in which they were, to give them protection, and in this position conducted them along. The Christians, finding themselves thus severely tried, and so worn out that they could bear up no longer, determined to continue their journey in the dark, thinking that they should be left alone on getting through the region of Quigualtam. While they proceeded and were least watchful, supposing themselves to be left, they would be roused with deafening yells near by: and thus were they annoyed through the night and until noon, when they got into another country, to the people of which they were recommended for a like treatment, and received it.

Those Indians having gone back to their country, these followed the Christians in fifty canoes, fighting them all one day and night. They sprang on board a brigantine of the rear-guard, by the canoe that floated at the stern, whence they took out an Indian woman, and wounded from thence some men in the brigantines. The men with the horses in the canoes, becoming weary with rowing day and night, at times got left behind, when the Indians would directly set upon them, and those in the brigantines would wait until they should come up: so that in consequence of the slow way that was made, because of the beasts, the Gov-

ernor determined to go on shore and slaughter
them. So soon as any befitting ground for it
was seen, a landing was made, the animals
were butchered, and the meat cured and
brought on board. Four or five horses having
been let go alive, the Indians, after the Spaniards had embarked, went up to them, to
whom being unused, they were alarmed, running up and down, neighing in such a way
that the Indians took fright, plunging into the
water; and thence entering their canoes, they
went after the brigantines, shooting at the
people without mercy, following them that
evening and the night ensuing, until ten
o'clock the next day, when they returned up
stream.

From a small town near the bank, there
came out seven canoes that pursued the Christians a short distance, shooting at them; but
finding, as they were few, that little harm was
done, they went back. From that time forth
the voyage, until near the end, was unattended
by any misadventure; the Christians in seven-
teen days going down a distance of two hundred and fifty leagues, a little more or less, by
the river. When near the sea, it becomes
divided into two arms, each of which may be
a league and a half broad.

CHAPTER XXXIX

HOW THE CHRISTIANS CAME TO THE SEA, WHAT OC-
CURRED THEN, AND WHAT BEFELL THEM ON THE
VOYAGE.

HALF a league before coming to the sea, the
Christians cast anchor, in order to take rest
for a time, as they were weary from rowing.
They were disheartened also, many days having gone by since they had eaten other thing
than maize, parched and then boiled, given
out in daily rations of a casque by strake [1] to a
mess of three.

While riding at anchor, seven canoes of natives came to attack those we had brought in
the canoes along with us. The Governor
ordered men to enter ours in armour, to go
after the Indians and drive them away.
There also came some by land, through thicket
and bog, with staves, having very sharp heads
of fish-bone, who fought valiantly those of us
who went out to meet them. Such as were
in the canoes, awaited with their arrows the
approach of those sent against them; and presently, on the engaging of these, as well as
those on land, they wounded some on our side
in both contests. When we on shore drew

[1] " Hũ casco arrasado," " a casque scraped," *i. e.,*
level full.   (B.)

nigh to them they would turn their backs, running like fleet steeds before infantry, making some turns without ever getting much beyond the flight of an arrow, and, returning again, they would shoot without receiving any injury from us, who, though we had some bows, were not skilled to use them; while the Indians on the water, finding their pursuers unable to do them harm, though straining at the oars to overtake them, leisurely kept within a circle, their canoes pausing and returning, as in a skirmish. The men discovered that the more successful their efforts to approach, the greater was their own injury; so, when they succeeded simply in driving them off, they went back to the brigantines.

After remaining two days, the Christians went to where that branch of the river enters the sea; and having sounded there, they found forty fathoms depth of water. Pausing then, the Governor required that each should give his opinion respecting the voyage, whether they should sail to New Spain direct, by the high sea, or go thither keeping along from shore to shore. There were different opinions upon this, in which Juan de Añasco, who was very presumptuous, valuing himself much upon his knowledge of navigation, with other matters of the sea of which he had little experience, influenced the Governor; and his opinion, like that of some others, was, that it would be much better to put out to sea, and cross the Gulf by a passage three-fourths less far, than going from shore to shore, which was very circuitous, because of the bend made by the land. He said that he had seen the sea-chart; that whence they were the coast ran west to the River of Palmas, and thence south to New Spain; consequently, that keeping in sight of land, there would be wide compassing, with long detention, and risk of being overtaken by the winter before coming to the country of Christians; while, with a fair wind, in ten or twelve days' time they should arrive there, by keeping a straight course.

The majority were not of that way of thinking, and said there was more safety in going along the coast, though it might take longer; the vessels being frail, and without decks, a light storm might suffice to wreck them; and in consequence of the little room they had for water, if calm or head wind should occur, or adverse weather, they would also run great hazard; but even were the vessels so substantial that they might venture in them, there being neither pilot nor sea-card to show the way, it was not wise to traverse the sea. This, the opinion of the greater number, was approved; and it was decided to go along from one to another shore.

When they were about to depart, the brigantine of the Governor parted her cable, the anchor attached to it remaining in the river; and, notwithstanding she was near the shore, the depth was so great that, although it was industriously sought for by divers, it could not be found. This gave much anxiety to the Governor and the others on board. With a stone for crushing maize, and the bridles that remained, belonging to some of the fidalgos and gentlemen who rode, they made a weight that took the place of the anchor.

On the eighteenth day of July the vessels got under weigh, with fair weather, and wind favourable for the voyage. The Governor, with Juan de Añasco, put to sea in their brigantines, and were followed by all the rest, who, at two or three leagues out, having come up with the two, the Captains asked the Governor why he did not keep the land; and told him that if he meant to leave it he should say so, though he ought not to do that without having the consent of the rest, otherwise they would not follow his lead, but each would do as he thought best. The Governor replied that he would do nothing without consulting them; he desired to get away from the shore to sail the better, and with the greater safety at night; that in the morning, when time served, he would return. With a favourable wind they sailed all that day in fresh water, the next night, and the day following until vespers, at which they were greatly amazed; for they were very distant from the shore, and so great was the strength of the current of the river, the coast so shallow and gentle, that the fresh water entered far into the sea.

That afternoon, on the starboard bow, they saw some kays, whither they went, and where they reposed at night. There Juan de Añasco, with his reasoning, concluded by getting all to consent, and deem it good, that they should go to sea, declaring, as he had before said, that it would be a great gain, and shorten their voyage. They navigated two days, and when they desired to get back in sight of land they could not, because the wind came off from it: and on the fourth day, finding that the water was giving out, fearing extremity and peril, they all complained of Juan de Añasco, and of the Governor, who had listened to his advice: and all the Captains declared they would run no farther out, and that the Governor might go as he chose.

It pleased God that the wind should change a little; and, at the end of four days from the time of their having gone out to sea, by strength of arm they arrived, in want of fresh water, in sight of the coast, and with great labour gained it on an open beach. That

afternoon, the wind came round from the
south, which on that coast is a side wind, and
so stiff that it threw the brigantines on to the
land, the anchors bending in their slenderness,
and dragging. The Governor ordered all to
leap into the water, on the larboard side, to
hold them, and when each wave had passed
they would launch the brigantines to seaward,
sustaining them in this manner until the wind
went down.

CHAPTER XL

How the Brigantines lost Sight of each other in
a Storm, and afterwards came together at a
Kay.

THE tempest having passed off from the
beach where the brigantines were riding, the
people went on shore. With mattocks they
dug holes there, into which the water having
flowed, they thence filled their pipkins. The
next day they left; and sailing two days, they
entered a basin, like a cove, which afforded
shelter against a high wind that blew from the
south. There they tarried, unable to leave,
until the fourth day, when the sea subsided
and they went out by rowing. They sailed
until near evening; the wind then freshened,
driving them in such manner upon the land,
that they regretted having left the harbour;

for no sooner was it nightfall than the storm began to rise on the sea, and with its approach the wind gradually increased. The brigantines separated. The two that were farthest out entered an arm of the sea, a couple of leagues beyond the place where the others found themselves at dark. The five that were astern remained from half a league to a league apart, along an exposed beach, upon which the winds and waves were casting them, without one vessel's knowing the fate of another. The anchors having yielded, the vessels were dragging them: the oars, at each of which seven and eight were pulling seaward, could not hold the vessels; the rest of the men, leaping into the water, with the utmost diligence, after the wave had passed that drove them to the shore, would launch the brigantine; while those on board, before another wave could come, baled out with bowls the water that came in upon them.

While thus engaged, in great fear of being lost, from midnight forward they suffered the intolerable torment of a myriad of mosquitos. The flesh is directly inflamed from their sting, as though it had received venom. Towards morning the wind lulled, and the sea went down; but the insects continued none the less. The sails, which were white, appeared black with them at daylight; while the men could not pull at the oars without assistance to drive away the insects. Fear having passed off with the danger of the storm, the people observing the swollen condition of each other's faces, and the marks of the blows they had given and received to rid them of the mosquitos, they could but laugh. The vessels came together in a creek, where lay the two brigantines that preceded them. Finding a scum the sea casts up, called copee, which is like pitch, and used instead on shipping, where that is not to be had, they payed the bottoms of their vessels with it.

After remaining two days they resumed their voyage; and having run likewise two days, they entered an arm of the sea and landed. Spending there a couple of days, they left; six men on the last day having gone up the bay in a canoe without finding its head. The brigantines went out in a head-wind blowing from the south, which being light, and the people having a strong desire to hasten the voyage, they pulled out by strength of arm to sea with great toil, and making little headway for two days, they entered by an arm of the sea behind an islet which it encircles, where followed such bad weather, that they were not unmindful to give thanks for that good shelter. Fish abounded there. They were taken in nets and with the line. A man hav-

ing thrown out a cord made fast to his arm, a
fish caught at the hook and drew him into
the water up to the neck, when, remembering
a knife that he had providentially kept, he
cut himself loose.

At the close of the fourteenth day of their
stay, the Almighty having thought proper to
send fair weather, the Christians very devoutly
formed a procession for the return of thanks,
in which, moving along the beach, they suppli-
cated Him that He would take them to a land
in which they might better do Him service.

CHAPTER   XLI

How the Christians arrived at the River Panico.

WHERESOEVER the people dug along the
shore they found fresh water.   The jars being
filled, and the procession concluded, they embarked; and, going ever in sight of land,
they navigated for six days.   Juan de Añasco
said it would be well to stand directly out to
sea; for that he had seen the card, and remembered that, from Rio de Palmas onward, the
coast ran south, and up to that time they had
gone westwardly.   According to his opinion,
by the reckoning he kept, the river could not
be distant from where we were.

That night they ran out, and in the morning

they saw palm-trees rising above the water, the coast trending southwardly; and from midday forward great mountains appeared, which had nowhere been seen until then; for to that place, from the port of Espiritu Santo, where they had entered Florida, was a low, level shore, not discoverable at sea until very near. From what they observed, they thought that during the night they had passed the Rio de Palmas, sixty leagues distant from Panico, in New Spain. So they consulted together.

Some were of opinion that it would not be well to sail in the dark, lest they should overrun the Rio de Panico; others, that they could not be so near as to run by it that night, and that it would not be well to lose a favourable wind; so they agreed to spread half the sails and keep on their way. Two of the brigantines, which ran with all sail up, at daylight passed the river without seeing it: of the five that remained behind, the first that arrived was the one Calderon commanded, from which, when a quarter of a league off, and before the entrance had been discovered, the water was observed to be thick and found to be fresh. Coming opposite the river, they saw where the waves broke upon a shoal, at the entrance into the sea; and, not any one knowing the place, they were in doubt whether they should go in there or pass by; but finally, having agreed to enter, they approached the shore without getting into the current, and went in the port, where no sooner had they come, than they saw Indians of both sexes in the apparel of Spain. Asking in what country they were, they received the answer in their own language, that it was the Rio de Panico, and that the town of the Christians was fifteen leagues inland. The pleasure that all received at this news cannot be sufficiently expressed: they felt as though a life had been newly given them. Many, leaping on shore, kissed the ground; and all, on bended knees, with hands raised above them, and their eyes to heaven, remained untiring in giving thanks to God.

Those who were coming astern, when they saw that Calderon with his brigantine had anchored in the river, directly steered to enter the port. The other two, which had gone by, tried to run to sea, that they might put about and join the rest, but could not, the wind being adverse and the sea fretful; so, fearing that they might be lost, they came nigh the land and cast anchor. A storm came up, and finding that they could not sustain themselves there, much less at sea, they determined to run on shore; and as the brigantines were small, drawing but little water, and the beach sandy, the force of the wind on the sails carried them up dry, without injury to any one.

If those who gained the haven at that time were made happy, these were oppressed by a double weight of gloom, not knowing what had happened to their companions, nor in what country they were, fearing likewise that it might be one of a hostile people. They had come upon the coast two leagues below the port. So soon as they found themselves clear of the sea, each took on the back what he could carry of his things, and, travelling inland, they found Indians, who told whence they were, and changed what was sorrow into joy. The Christians rendered many thanks to God for having rescued them from those numberless perils.

CHAPTER XLII

How the Christians came to Panico, and of their Reception by the Inhabitants.

From the time the Christians left the River Grande, to come by sea from Florida to the River of Panico, were fifty-two days. On the tenth day of September, of the year 1543, they entered the Panico, going up with the brigantines. In the many windings taken by the stream, the light wind was often unfavourable, and the vessels in many places made slow headway, having to be towed with much labour against a strong current; so that, after having sailed four days, the people, discovering themselves greatly retarded in the desire to get among Christians, and of taking part in the divine offices, which for a long season had not been listened to by them, they gave up the brigantines to the sailors, and went on by land to Panico.

Just as the Christians arrived at the town, in their clothing of deer-skin, dressed and dyed black, consisting of frock, hose, and shoes, they all went directly to the church, to pray and return thanks for their miraculous preservation. The townspeople, having already been informed of their coming by the Indians, and now knew of the arrival, invited some to their houses, and entertained them for acquaintance sake, or for having heard of them, or because they came from the same parts of country with themselves. The Alcalde-Mayor took the Governor home with him: the rest, as they came up, he directed to be lodged by sixes and tens, according to the means of individuals, who provided their guests with abundance of fowls and maizen-bread, and with the fruits of the country, which are like those of Cuba, already described.

The town of Panico might contain some

seventy housekeepers. The dwellings were
chiefly of stone and mortar; some were of
poles, and all of them thatched with grass.
The country is poor. No gold or silver is to
be found. Residents have the fullest supply
both of food and servants. The most wealthy
have not an income above five hundred cruzados annually, which is tribute paid by their
Indian vassals, in cotton clothing, fowls, and
maize.

Of the persons who got back from Florida,
there landed at that port three hundred and
eleven Christians. The Alcalde-Mayor directly sent a townsman by post to inform the
Viceroy, who resided in Mexico, of the arrival of three hundred of the men who had
gone with Don Hernando de Soto in the
discovery and conquest of Florida; and, for
their being in the service of the King, that he
would make provision for their support. Don
Antonio de Mendoza was greatly amazed at
this news, as were all others of that city;
for the people having entered far into Florida,
they had been considered lost, nothing being
heard from them in a long while; and it
appeared to him to be a thing impossible, that
without a fortress to which they might betake
themselves, or support of any sort, they should
have sustained themselves for such a length
of time among the heathen. He immediately

gave an order, directing that subsistence should be given them wheresoever it might be needed, and the Indians found requisite for carrying their burdens; and, should there be refusal, to take by force, without incurring any penalty, whatsoever should be necessary. The mandate was so well obeyed, that on the road, before the people had arrived at the towns, the inhabitants went out to receive them, bringing fowls and provisions.

CHAPTER XLIII

THE FAVOUR THE PEOPLE FOUND IN THE VICEROY AND RESIDENTS OF MEXICO.

FROM Panico to the great city of Mestitam, Mexico, there are sixty leagues, and as many leagues from each to the port of Vera Cruz, which is where the embarkations take place for Spain, and where those who go hence to New Spain arrive. These three towns, equidistant, are inhabited by Spaniards, and form a triangle: Vera Cruz on the south, Panico on the east, and Mexico, which is inland, on the west. The country is so populous, that the Indian towns farthest apart are not more than half a league to a league from each other.

Some of the people who came from Florida

remained in Panico, reposing a month, others
fifteen days, or such time as each pleased; for
no one turned a grudging face to his guest,
but, on the contrary, gave him of every thing
he had, and appeared sad at his leave-taking;
which may well enough be believed, for the
provision the natives brought in payment of
their tribute more than sufficed for consumption, so that there was no one in that town to
buy or to sell, and few Spaniards being there,
the inhabitants were glad of company. All
the clothing in the custody of the Alcalde-
Mayor, paid to him there as the Emperor's
tax, he divided among those that would go to
receive any.

He who had a coat of mail was happy, since
for it a horse might be had in exchange. Some
got mounted, and those not able to get beasts,
who were the greater number, took up the
journey on foot. They were well received
by the Indians, and better served than they
could have been at their own homes, particularly in respect of every thing to eat; for,
if an Indian was asked for a fowl, he would
bring four; and if for any sort of fruit,
though it might be a league off, some one
would run to fetch it; and were a Christian
ill, the people would carry him, in a chair,
from their own to the next town. Wheresoever they came, the Cacique of the place,

through an Indian who bears a rod of justice in his hand they call tapile (which is equivalent to saying meirinho), ordered provisions to be brought, and men for the loads of such things as they were, and the others necessary to carry the invalids.

The Viceroy sent a Portugues to them, twenty leagues from Mexico, with quantity of confections, raisins, pomegranates, and other matters proper for the sick, should they need them; and, in advance, ordered that all should be clothed at the royal charge. The news of their approach being known to the citizens, they went out on the highway to receive them, and with great courtesy entreated for their companionship as favour, each one taking to his house as many as he dared, giving them for raiment all the best he could, the least well dressed wearing clothes worth thirty cruzados and upward. Clothing was given to those who chose to go for it to the residence of the Viceroy, and the persons of condition ate at his board: at his house was a table for all those of less rank that would eat there. Directly he informed himself of the quality of each one, that he might show him the consideration that was his due. Some of the Conquistadores placed them all down to table together, fidalgos and boors, oftentimes seating the servant and his master shoulder to shoulder; which was done mostly by artisans and men of mean condition, those better bred asking who each one was, and making a difference in persons.

Nevertheless, all did the best they could with good will, telling those they had under their roofs that they could bring no impoverishment, nor should they hesitate to receive whatsoever they offered; since they had found themselves in like condition when others had assisted them, such being the fortunes of the country. God reward them: and those whom He saw fit should escape, coming out of Florida to tread the soil of Christians, be He pleased that they live to serve Him; and to the dead, and to all those who believe in Him, and confess that in Him is their faith, grant, through His compassion, the glory of paradise. Amen.

CHAPTER XLIIII

WHICH SETS FORTH SOME OF THE DIVERSITIES AND
PECULIARITIES OF FLORIDA; AND THE FRUIT,
BIRDS, AND BEASTS OF THE COUNTRY.

FROM the port of Espiritu Santo, where the Christians went on shore, to the Province of Ocute, which may be a distance of four hundred leagues, a little more or less, the country is very level, having many ponds, dense thickets, and, in places, tall pine-trees: the soil is light, and there is not in it a mountain nor a hill.

The land of Ocute is more strong and fertile than the rest, the forest more open; and it has very good fields along the margins of the rivers. From there to Cutifachiqui are about one hundred and thirty leagues, of which eighty leagues are of desert and pine forests, through which run great rivers. From Cutifachiqui to Xuala there may be two hundred and fifty leagues, and all a country of mountains: the places themselves are on high level ground, and have good fields upon the streams.

Thence onward, through Chiaha, Coça, and Talise, the country of which is flat, dry, and strong, yielding abundance of maize, to Tascaluça, may be two hundred and fifty leagues; and thence to Rio Grande, a distance of about three hundred leagues, the land is low, abounding in lakes. The country afterward is higher, more open, and more populous than any other in Florida; and along the River Grande, from Aquixo to Pacaha and Coligoa, a distance of one hundred and fifty leagues, the land is level, the forest open, and in places the fields very fertile and inviting.

From Coligoa to Autiamque may be two

hundred and fifty leagues of mountainous
country; thence to Guacay may be two hundred and thirty leagues of level ground; and
the region to Daycao, a distance of one hundred and twenty leagues, is continuously of
mountainous lands.

From the port of Espiritu Santo to Apalache they marched west and northeast; from
Cutifachiqui to Xuala, north; to Coça, westwardly; and thence to Tascaluça and the
River Grande, as far as the Provinces of
Quizquiz and Aquixo, to the westward; from
thence to Pacaha northwardly, to Tula westwardly, to Autiamque southwardly, as far as
the Province of Guachoya and Daycao.

The bread that is eaten all through Florida
is made of maize, which is like coarse millet;
and in all the islands and Indias belonging
to Castilla, beginning with the Antillas, grows
this grain. There are in the country many
walnuts likewise, and *ameixas,* mulberries,
and grapes. The maize is planted and picked
in, each person having his own field; fruit
is common for all, because it grows abundantly in the woods, without any necessity
of setting out trees or pruning them. Where
there are mountains the chestnut is found, the
fruit of which is somewhat smaller than the
one of Spain. Westward of the Rio Grande
the walnut differs from that which is found

before coming there, being of tenderer shell, and in form like an acorn; while that behind, from the river back to the port of Espiritu Santo, is generally rather hard, the tree and the nut being in their appearance like those of Spain. There is everywhere in the country a fruit, the produce of a plant like ligoacam, that is propagated by the Indians, having the appearance of the royal pear, with an agreeable smell and taste; and likewise another plant, to be seen in the fields, bearing a fruit like strawberry, near to the ground, and is very agreeable. The *ameixas* are of two sorts, vermilion and gray, of the form and size of walnuts, having three or four stones in them. They are better than any plums that are raised in Spain, and make much better prunes. The grapes appear only to need dressing; for, although large, they have great stones; the other fruits are all in great perfection, and are less unhealthy than those of Spain.

There are many lions and bears in Florida, wolves, deer, jackals, cats, and conies; numerous wild fowl, as large as pea-fowl; small partridges, like those of Africa, and cranes, ducks, pigeons, thrushes, and sparrows. There are blackbirds larger than sparrows and smaller than stares; hawks, goss-hawks, falcons, and all the birds of rapine to be found in Spain.

The Indians are well proportioned: those of the level country are taller and better shaped of form than those of the mountains; those of the interior enjoy a greater abundance of maize and clothing than those of the coast, where the land is poor and thin, and the people along it more warlike.

The direction from the port of Espiritu Santo to Apalache, and thence to Rio de las Palmas, is from east to west; from that river towards New Spain, it is southwardly; the sea-coast being gentle, having many shoals and high sand-hills.

DEO GRATIAS.

THIS Relation of the Discovery of Florida was impressed in the house of Andree de Burgos, Printer and Cavalleiro of the house of Senhor Cardinal iffante.

It was finished the tenth day of February, of the year one thousand five hundred and fifty-seven, in the noble and ever loyal city of Evora.